THE
brighter marketing bible

THE
brighter marketing bible

joanne morley | siobhan lees

LEANMARKETING™
★PRESS★

First Published In Great Britain 2009
by Lean Marketing Press
www.BookShaker.com

Typeset in Book Antiqua

Praise

"I don't read many books but The Brighter Marketing Bible is great. Joanne and Siobhan have a down to earth attitude to marketing that gives you the inside knowledge you really need to make your marketing work for you. What's more it's not packed full of theory, its stuff that has actually worked for them in the past."

Vin Maguire – Managing Director Sec-1

"I have only been working in a marketing role for over a year, but I have found the information in this book invaluable. It gives you the practical knowledge you need and their step by step approach means you gain information quickly and easily. I wouldn't be without it."

Pavan Gata-Aura – Marketing Officer

"Joanne and Siobhan's approach to marketing really makes you think about what you are doing and more importantly why you are doing it. They get under the skin of what people are really buying, and as we found out, it's not our products and services."

Simon Fisher – Managing Director Ware4

"Some of the information in this book is completely obvious, but that's what makes it so good. Many of us think that we know how to market our products and services, but sometimes we just need reminding what we aren't doing and how small changes could make a big difference to the success of our marketing campaigns."

Suzanne Burnett – Managing Director, Castle Employment Agency

"Read this book, do what they tell you to do and you will get results, I wish I had read this sooner."
Steve Lightfoot – Managing Director, Pudsey Computers

"What I liked was Joanne and Siobhan's energy and enthusiasm for marketing, they want you to succeed and have given you all the knowledge you need to do this. There is very little jargon and they have a really straightforward approach to marketing."
Jon Wigley – Founder and Managing Director, And Business Coaching

"If you are stuck in a marketing rut, buy this book."
Logan Anderson – Head of Customer Relations, The Pensions Trust

"I liked this book because it was simple, easy to read and most of all gave me the marketing knowledge I needed to make my marketing more successful."
Kelly Lynch – Business Development Manager, Addleshaw Goddard

Contents

Who Are We and Why Should You Believe What We Say?

We are Siobhan Lees and Joanne Morley, co-directors of Brighter Marketing Ltd, a company we established in 2002 to provide marketing help, support and guidance through a unique coaching-based approach that helps our clients improve their businesses through effective marketing.

Before we set up Brighter Marketing, we worked in senior sales and marketing roles in a range of business-to-business (B2B) companies, some large, some small. These companies had one thing in common: much of their success was due to effective marketing that had to deliver results. Working in high-pressure environments meant we had to devise marketing campaigns that worked and delivered high-quality sales leads on a regular basis. And, for a number of years, that's what we both did - we set up marketing systems that provided consistent enquiries that ultimately led to sales revenue.

We have been in your situation. We have had our backs against the wall and had to create effective marketing programmes. We have felt the pressure, we understand what it's like. But we also know it doesn't have to be like that. Time has been a great teacher for both of us and, if we had only known then what we know now, perhaps we wouldn't have needed that towel to continually wipe the sweat from our brow.

This book has been written to help you reduce your stress levels and to save you the time and money you may currently be ploughing into marketing that doesn't seem to work, no matter how much you put in. Its goal is to give you the knowledge and tools you need to develop a highly effective marketing approach that can help you achieve the results you want from marketing.

If you are looking for SWOTS, PESTLE analysis and Boston Consulting matrices, you won't find them here - just real-life marketing ideas, tips and guidance that will get results.

Why Did We Write The Book?

There are lots of marketing books out there. Many are based on theory that would never work in the real world, and we should know - we read most of them in the course of our marketing careers!

When we started Brighter Marketing, we were on a mission to provide the best marketing support, help and guidance we could to make our clients' businesses successful. And we soon realised that providing marketing plans wasn't the most effective way forward. What our clients needed was:

1. To understand how marketing could help give them the business they wanted
2. To be part of the process and learn from our experience of what works and what doesn't, so they could implement the right marketing campaigns in the future
3. Results! They needed their marketing to work for them and their businesses and to deliver quality sales leads and enquiries.

We offered an approach that was different to that of many of our competitors. We knew a coaching and mentoring service would be a more effective way of transferring the key marketing skills our clients needed.

Of course, not everyone wanted to work with us in this way, so we developed some articles outlining the basics of marketing that could be downloaded from our website (*www.brightermarketing.com*). Then, as demand for the downloads grew, we realised there was an audience for what we had to say - and so this book was born. We wanted to share our knowledge with others, so that they could make a difference to how they marketed their products and services.

We also invited over 800 subscribers to our e-bulletin to tell us about their biggest marketing challenges, to ensure the book was an accurate reflection of the marketing challenges you face. The response was great and, where possible, we have incorporated answers to these challenges throughout the book. Our thanks to all the people who responded - you made us think and, ultimately, make this an even more practical book than we first envisaged.

Foreword

As a wealth coach I've been lucky enough to help many people turn their business ideas into six and seven figure incomes. I could list success stories in vastly different fields - coaches, consultants, information publishers, trainers, property developers, accountants, artists, musicians, dentists - the list goes on. Yet, no matter what route they take to making their fortune one thing remains constant. The need for a well planned and expertly implemented marketing strategy.

The real challenge is that many people start out on their path to business success as solo-preneurs, with limited resources, limited time and often, in the case of marketing, limited knowledge. Well this book plugs that essential gap by providing you with a brimful of easy-to-implement marketing approaches that have been used successfully by the authors to promote their own growing marketing firm and drive the success of their many grateful clients.

In essence, what Siobhan and Joanne have done so well in this book is to generously share many of their insider tricks, tips and tactics so that you can accelerate your understanding and application of a properly formulated strategic marketing plan.

So, I urge you to grab this opportunity to learn from these two marketing experts and then go out and make your fortune too.

Nicola Cairncross
Wealth Coach, Professional Speaker and Author of "The Money Gym"
www.themoneygym.com

How To Use This Book

Hello, and thank you for purchasing this invaluable marketing resource that will revolutionise the way you approach your business-to-business marketing.

The book has been written from a UK perspective. However, these marketing principles apply wherever you are in the world. We have considered other markets and, where applicable, have included references to them.

You may not want to read the book chapter by chapter, so just dip in and read the chapters you believe are most relevant to you. However, we recommend you do read *Chapters 1* and *2* which are all about getting your mind fit for marketing and setting your goals. It is vitally important to do this before you undertake any marketing activity, as it ensures you know where you are heading and that you initiate the most appropriate marketing activity to get you there.

JUICY BITS

Then, if you want to get to the juiciest bits - the marketing activities, tips and techniques - read *Chapter 7*. A word of warning: you must have a perfectly clear picture of who you are targeting. You can develop the most amazing marketing campaign, but if it is focused on the wrong companies and individuals, all your effort will have been wasted. *Chapter 4* helps you to define who you are selling to, to ensure your marketing activities are focused like a laser beam on the right audience.

1. How You Can Affect Your Marketing Results

"If you keep on doing things like you've always done, what you'll get is what you've already got."
ANON

Any journey has to begin from a starting point: before you know where you want to be, you have to know where you are now.

Do any of these statements relate to your business?

- ☐ There is a reduction in sales enquiries
- ☐ Competitors are taking clients away
- ☐ Marketing costs are increasing but sales leads are decreasing
- ☐ Tried and tested marketing activities just aren't working any more
- ☐ There is a lack of consistency in your marketing materials
- ☐ Your brand looks old and tired
- ☐ You have new products and services but haven't had the time to promote them effectively
- ☐ You have grown, but your employees all have different ideas of what you do
- ☐ You're not sure which marketing tools to use and which would be the most effective
- ☐ You are too busy to think about marketing
- ☐ There is reduced marketing effort due to workload
- ☐ Marketing just isn't working, you don't know why you bother

At least one of these is bound to apply to you. These are the kind of things our clients complain about when we first meet them. They are stuck in a marketing rut and don't know how to get out of it. They want us to wave a magic wand and make it all better. If we could, we would, but we find that the first place to look to if you want to improve your marketing is…

YOU

Well, you must be reading this book for a reason!

OPEN YOUR MIND - ACHIEVE GREAT THINGS

For you to achieve great things with marketing, you and your team must have the right mindset. Start by looking in the mirror. It is important to understand we all have a set of…

- Beliefs
- Boundaries
- Constraints
- Attitudes
- Perceptions

…and have been conditioned to think in a certain way.

All of these shape our view of marketing and what it can do for us. For example, if you believe marketing is about brochures, sales letters, cold calling and flyers, this is what you will focus on. Your mind won't be receptive to the idea of setting up a blog on the internet because this doesn't fit into the thoughts you hold about other marketing tools.

Before moving forward, you need to understand what your beliefs, constraints, etc, are about marketing, so you can acknowledge them and, if necessary, change them to ensure your mind is open to the massive range of tools and techniques that can be considered under the heading of "marketing".

Look at the following image. What do you see?

Most people see strange and meaningless black shapes, because our minds are conditioned to look at black shapes and figures. You have probably ignored the white shapes between the black ones, which is where the real meaning in this diagram lies.

Here's what else you can see in the image...

If you look at the white shapes you will see two words emerging:

'FLY' and 'WIN'

Once you see them, the white shapes become dominant and the black shapes recede.

Here is another one, taken from *'Thinker Toys'*, a book on creativity by Michael Michalko...

"Some years ago, a group of scientists visited a tribe in New Guinea who believed that their world ended at a nearby river. After several months, one of the scientists had to leave, which involved crossing the river. Safely across the river he turned and waved. The tribesmen did not respond because, they said, they didn't see him. Their entrenched beliefs about the world had distorted their perception of reality."

GET FIT FOR MARKETING

It is essential that you are familiar with your and your team's perceptions and beliefs about marketing, as they could be one of the biggest blockages to you achieving great results. List all the negative things you believe about marketing, or assumptions that might be holding you back. Then substitute them with positive assumptions that will ensure you start from a positive point of view. We have given you one to get started and there is a template that you can complete for yourself.

NEGATIVE BELIEF	POSITIVE BELIEF
Producing another direct mail campaign is pointless. The last one bombed and we got no response from it, even though we worked really hard and spent a lot of time and effort on it.	This is all-or-nothing thinking. The next direct mail we develop could produce amazing results (if I look at the tips later in this book – it should!) All we need to do is be a little more creative and open up our minds to new ideas of what direct mail is and how it really works.

Complete this to ensure you are in a marketing-ready mindset:

NEGATIVE BELIEF	POSITIVE BELIEF

MARKETING MOTIVATION

One of the questions we were asked when we were writing this book was:

"How do we get motivated to carry out marketing activities when other priorities seem to be more pressing?"

The question you have to ask yourself is: "Why are you not motivated to carry out marketing activities?"

Have you completed the exercise on the previous page to identify any negative beliefs you have about marketing that might be holding you back?

Marketing doesn't really work – does it?

In the dark recesses of your mind, you might actually be thinking there is no point in doing another direct mail because the last one bombed. If you believe this, work on banishing this and other negative thoughts about marketing. Think about the positive things marketing can do for your company. Read some of the chapters that cover points you want to know more about. Identify areas where you can improve and motivate yourself to achieve much more. Read *Chapter 2*, set some marketing objectives and be sure to plan them using the handy schedules we've included.

Taking multi-tasking to the extreme

If the real reason you can't get motivated to carry out marketing activities is because it means taking multi-tasking to the Olympic Gold standard, stop! Think about what you want to achieve with your marketing - *Chapter 2* will help - and work out if a) you are aiming too high and need to scale things down a bit, or b) you need some extra help. If the answer is b, get the help. If you want your marketing approach to succeed, you need to have the resources to achieve your goals.

You may also find the book *'Focus: The Power of Targeted Thinking'* by Jurgen Wolff useful as it gives tips and techniques on how to remain focused on your goals.

MOTIVATED – BUT SOME THINGS STILL IRRITATING YOU?

Now that your mind is fit and ready for marketing, what do you do about all those things that irritate you about your marketing approach: lack of sales leads, competition winning business from you, or your lack-lustre brand? The answer is to write them down, so that you know what they are and can address them, rather than just letting them run around in your head. Go on, write down the ten things that are really annoying you about your marketing right now:

Put your list to one side and you can revisit it once you have read the book. By reading the advice in the following chapters you will begin to see why certain marketing campaigns didn't work or why things have been irritating you.

2. Where Do You Want To Be?

"The reason most people never reach their goals is that they don't define them, or ever seriously consider them as believable or achievable…
…Winners can tell you where they are going, what they plan to do along the way, and who will be sharing the adventure with them."
DENIS WATLEY

We looked at where you are now in the previous chapter. If you didn't cover this, have a quick look back to confirm that you are ready to take on the marketing challenge and that your mind is full of positive thoughts around marketing.

Where do you want to be? You know your starting point, but imagine setting off on a journey, not really knowing where you are headed, or where you really want to go. You might end up somewhere really nice, if you are lucky, and find a map stuffed under the seat. Or you might get lost and end up in a less than desirable neighbourhood with no way out!

Many of the companies we have worked with have found themselves in just such a place: with a business that isn't in a great position, with seemingly no way out and declining revenues. In many cases, they think the answer to their prayers is a new logo, brochure or a direct mail. That will bring in new clients and save the day. Won't it?

The answer is no! Throwing money at a new brochure if you don't know where you are going is a complete waste. Firstly, how do you know if a brochure or direct mail is what you need, if you don't know where you are going? And, secondly, what are you going to promote if you yourself aren't clear about what your company wants to achieve?

Stop! You need to get focused and know where you are heading before you undertake even one more marketing activity.

GET FOCUSED – RIGHT NOW!

If there is one thing you must do before you start any marketing, it is to decide where you want to be. It sounds simple – and it is – the vision for the business will be key in determining the marketing strategy and tactics you need to deploy to achieve your goal.

It is also vitally important that this is communicated throughout the company. If your employees don't know where you are heading, how can they help you get there? Everyone will pull in different directions and your marketing won't be effective.

Remember, marketing is the responsibility of everyone (not just the marketing department), from the way the phones are answered to how the sales team approaches selling. All of this builds up an image in the minds of prospects and of your clients. If employees deliver consistent messages, great! If not, much of your marketing effort can go to waste.

Goals are critical to your business's success. They keep you and your team focused and ensure the marketing you undertake keeps you on the right track to achieve them.

So, discuss your goals for the business with your team. Here are some questions to get your session started and to stimulate thoughts and ideas. This is not about creating a mission statement - it is about putting a stake in the ground, defining who you are, what you do and what you want your company to become.

- What kind of company are we?
- What are we selling?
- Who are we selling it to?
- What do we want to achieve in the next year, two years, etc?
- Why do we want it?
- What is our ultimate goal?
- What do we want our clients to think about us?

You need a clear picture of what you want to achieve to ensure your marketing can help you do it.

If one of your goals is to grow the business by 20% over the next three years and then sell it, this will require a different marketing approach than a company that wants to increase sales by 5% year-on-year.

Write it down

Write down your goals. Studies show that commitments that are made actively have more staying power than those made passively. In the book *Focus: The Power of Targeted Thinking*, the author states that many successful people say they write down their goals instead of just thinking about them. Look at your goals every day and spend some time trying to achieve them.

IF THEY DON'T KNOW WHERE YOU'RE GOING, HOW CAN THEY FOLLOW?

Once you know what your goals are, write them down and communicate them to every person in the organisation so that everyone knows what they are and can work with you to commit to achieving them. Marketing does not provide the magic solution to achieving them all, but it can go a long way. As we said previously, marketing is everyone's responsibility and, if employees know where you are heading, they can do their bit to make sure you get there.

Print out your goals and look at them every day to make sure that you are working towards achieving them and, if necessary, amend or adjust them as things change. If you look at them every day, your mind becomes focused on achieving them and filters out thoughts that won't help you to get where you want to go.

HOW MARKETING CAN HELP YOU ACHIEVE YOUR GOALS

If you know what you want to achieve at a company level, how can marketing help you get there? The easiest way is to brainstorm all the areas where marketing can have an impact on your business. We have suggested a few for you; you can probably think of more.

Filter them down to five or six key areas where marketing could have a positive impact on helping you achieve your overall goals and set yourself a marketing objective.

Here are some areas you may want to consider:

To get you started, we have provided a table on the following page which you can complete with your marketing objectives. We have pre-filled the first entry for you so you can see how it works. Do take time to fill in the rest of your marketing objectives: they will help ensure that your marketing stays on track.

So the next time you receive a call from an advertising sales executive offering you an amazing discount on advertising in the local paper, you can look at your goals and see if his readership fits your target market. If it doesn't, the answer is simple: "No thanks, my target market doesn't read that publication". See how easy it is to stop wasting money?

AREA OF FOCUS	MARKETING OBJECTIVE
Target Market	Identify IT Managers in organisations with over 100 employees in the North of the UK who have over £100k IT budget. These are the most likely source of revenue for the business and we aim to gain 20 new customers this year with an average revenue of £10,000 per customer.

3. What Are You Actually Selling?

"Art is making something out of nothing and then selling it."
FRANK ZAPPA

It's a fairly simple question, but an important one, that you need to answer right now, before you go any further.

What are you selling? List the things you sell:

That's great. You know what products you are selling and, if you are a company selling mechanical diggers, your list probably looks something like this:

1. Mini Diggers

2. Wheeled Excavators

3. Tracked Diggers

4. Micro Diggers

However, there are two ways of looking at your products and services. The first way is to talk about the physical product and to sell the features and benefits of the product. This is OK, but it doesn't really make your marketing message stand out.

That's why your perfectly designed information sheets which talk about the features of the digger, the speed at which it digs and the special bucket it has that makes digging easier, are great as a technical specification. Websites full of digger pictures and specs eventually merge into one for a prospective client, making it difficult for them to choose between one company and another.

Of course, it is important to be very clear about the range of products and services you sell and, if you do sell diggers to the building industry, focus on what you do best and provide the best diggers possible for your clients.

However, sometimes it is worth thinking about another angle to marketing your products and services - one that many business-to-business companies completely ignore: emotion and expertise.

EMOTION – THE HIDDEN MARKETING SECRET

It is important to remember you are selling to people, not companies or machines. People are emotional beings; they don't just start operating on logic as soon as they walk through the door into work. Whether you or they realise it, your prospective clients use a balance of emotion and logic to buy from you, just as they did when they went out and made an emotional decision to buy a BMW rather than a Honda. If you want to succeed in marketing, you have to appeal to their emotions.

While diggers may be the products you sell, what you are actually selling is often something entirely different. Many of our clients become resistant at this point. Perhaps you are, too. But if your mind is fully primed and ready to learn something new, this chapter will give you all the ammunition you need to turbo-charge your marketing. Consider this:

> *"No one who bought a mechanical digger actually wants*
> *a digger; they want a great big hole in the ground or to*
> *move some earth around to allow them to build a house!"*

Think about it. It's true. If you can appeal to their emotions and provide information around how your diggers create the best holes in the business, in the least amount of time and can save them thousands of £s or $s in excavation costs, the digger just becomes the thing that gives them what they really want.

Elizabeth Arden, whose retail business is well known in the consumer world, can teach B2B companies something. She knew how to make her customers buy from her time and time again. She realised that…

> *"I don't sell cosmetics, I sell hope."*

She knew every pot of cream, lipstick, lotion or potion she created gave women hope - hope that their wrinkles would disappear; hope that the new lipstick would make them look just like the model who was advertising it; hope that, somehow, by using her products, they would look great.

When you look at things from a different perspective, you begin to see that what you are really selling is something quite different to the physical product or service.

And you can strengthen this even further by making yourself the expert who creates these amazing products - people will be beating a path to your door. Before we move on to that, do one or more of these simple exercises to help you think more creatively about the marketing messages you can use to support your business.

PERCEPTION IS THE WINNER, NOT PRODUCTS & SERVICES

Jack Trout and Al Ries, authors of *'The 22 Immutable Laws of Marketing'*, make the following statement:

"Marketing is not a battle of products but a battle of perceptions"

To make your business a success, you must work on how your company is perceived by clients and potential clients. You need to understand what you are really selling and that better perceptions about your company will always win, no matter how great your product is.

THREE WAYS TO MAKE SURE YOUR CUSTOMERS KNOW WHAT YOU ARE SELLING

The first thing to do when trying to establish what you are really selling is to set aside at least a couple of hours with the rest of the team to explore all the possible reasons people buy from you.

We have devised some exercises to use in your session to draw out emotional reasons why people buy products and services from you. If you have a large number of products or services, consider breaking them down into ranges or key areas to make it easier.

1 – Power Messages

List all the things your product or service can do for your clients using these six keywords:

Increase	Save	Gain
Enhance	Reduce	Improve

These are powerfully emotive words and they serve as the impetus to get you thinking. If you sell technical IT training, your power messages could be:

- Increase your confidence
- Gain new skills
- Reduce your stress
- Save time taken to complete routine network tasks
- Improve your networking skills

Use your imagination, get creative and produce as many ideas as you can. Write down the keywords first, e.g., Increase your confidence. You can work on completing the message once you have decided what keywords to use. For example:

- **Increase your confidence** with proven IT training skills that allow you to solve network problems quickly.

- **Gain new skills.** In just two days, you will have the knowledge you need to keep your network up and running 99.9% of the time.

- **Reduce the stress** associated with network downtime and learn how to spot issues before they arise.

- **Reduce the time taken to complete routine network tasks** with our specialised training that shows you the fast-track way to maintaining your network.

2 – In Your Client's Shoes

This exercise encourages you to think like your client. People spend a lot of time thinking about what they want to communicate to clients rather than thinking about what clients actually need, or want.

Get a large piece of paper, draw round a pair of shoes, write "client's shoes" on it and put it on the floor. Each team member should take turns to stand "in" the shoes and answer the following questions. It might sound strange, but putting yourself in the client's shoes seems to produce better results than if you just imagine wearing them while you sit round the table. You can add more questions, but these should be enough to get started:

- Why did you buy from us?
- What was it you liked about our product/service?
- Why did you choose this product and not another product?
- What was most important to you when choosing a company to work with?
- What did you think of the competition?
- What did we do really well?
- What's the most important aspect of your job?
- How did we help you?
- What were your requirements?

Take a good look at the answers. Are they what you expected? Did you really put yourself in the client's shoes? If you did, you should have some useful information that will help you understand what you are really selling - it should be about more than just the features of the product.

3 – Ask Your Clients

In this exercise, you need to actually call your clients and ask them why they bought from you. You can use the same questions you asked in the previous exercise. If you want frank, honest answers, consider using someone independent to ask the questions - your clients are likely to be more honest in their responses than they would if they were talking directly to you.

To find the reasons individuals really buy from you, you need to turn things inside out. The real gems are in your client's minds.

Take time to define what you are really selling and to identify the emotional triggers that make your clients want to buy from you, not just once, but time and time again.

4 – Client Needs-analysis

Once you have this information, you could use the matrix on the following page to develop marketing messages. It works by asking a series of questions to make you think about what clients really want.

Here is a sample client's needs analysis based on a new service from an accountancy firm that allowed clients to log in to their accounts information remotely:

Key Issues or frustrations	How important is this and why?	How would overcoming this help?	Their requirements	What can Newsol deliver?
How much is it going to cost?	If they think it is going to be a costly exercise, they may be put off. Also, is cost the only reason stopping them from working with Newsol.	Fairness and equity in pricing. Easier for them to budget using Newsol into their costs and ability to calculate the savings.	Fixed, fair prices that are quoted up-front and are broken down and easy to understand.	All costs clearly defined in advance for financial services provided. The cost of using Newsol is recovered through reduced financial and accountancy costs.
Not enough proactive financial advice or help with running the business.	If they think they are just getting a technology based service they may worry that they will lose the advice they get from their accountants.	Talk, educate and show them how Newsol can add real value to business performance with advice and best practice support.	Want to feel that they fully understand the benefits of working with Newsol and what it can do for them.	A persuasive and educative approach to selling that is not prescriptive and works with the client's financial situation.
What can you do for me?	Open-ended question but they are asking for help.	They must easily understand the services available from Newsol so they can match them to their needs.	Easy-to-understand service with clear benefits.	Marketing collateral and website that clearly defines the solution and the benefits.
Accountants take a long time to deliver their services. Why are you different?	Accountants can slow down the year-end accounts, etc, so clients feel they don't have a good view of their overall financial position.	Effective management of their financial processes will save them time and reduce their costs.	Clear definition of how information is processed and the provision of accounts to help with financial planning and cash flow.	Guaranteed access to financial information, KPIs that will help them run their business more efficiently.
Too many contacts at my accountants - I never know who I should be speaking to.	Consistency of advice and continuity is important; the client wants to feel valued and that they are not just another low-level client.	If they have only one contact, they always know who to turn to for support when they need it. Things won't fall through the cracks.	Single point of contact who knows everything about their requirements. Can help with understanding financial reports, etc.	Senior point of contact who is involved in the set-up and delivery of the accounts process and advice from the outset.
I am worried about the security of my financial information if I outsource.	The security of financial information will be very important to clients. They will want complete assurances that their information is kept safe and secure.	Providing assurances that data protection and the online security of the information will be vital to overcoming this fear.	They want to know that the information is secure and no other individuals can gain access to it.	A highly secure process that provides more security and back-up processes than they currently have on their own premises. So information will be safer with Newsol.

WHAT REALLY GOES ON IN YOUR CLIENT'S MIND?

By thinking like your clients and asking them why they buy from you, you will build up a pretty clear picture of what is going on in their minds. However, there may be a few things they won't tell you; not because they don't want to, but because they probably haven't realised themselves why they selected you.

Here are some general examples you may want to consider:

- **You made them look good.** You provided a product or service that helped them to gain a positive reputation in their company. For example, a design agency develops a direct mail piece that delivers a large number of leads - the marketing manager not only feels great but is commended for delivering a good return on investment.
- **You increased their knowledge and skills.** They could undertake their role with more confidence.
- **You made them feel successful.** Your product or service enabled them to succeed in their role.
- **You made their job easier.** You enabled them to go home at 5pm on Fridays instead of working late.
- **You gave them perspective.** You took them out of a situation and gave them the opportunity to see their challenge or problem from a different viewpoint.
- **You valued them, their ideas and opinions.** This can be quite important, especially if their colleagues have ignored their ideas.
- **You gave them motivation and security.** They took on a complex challenge which they didn't want to attempt on their own.
- **You listened to them, gave them some attention.** If no one is listening to their concerns or frustrations, the time you spend with them can be invaluable.
- **You gave them insight.** You enabled them to gain an insight into their challenge that they couldn't see for all the company politics, etc.
- **You helped and supported them.** You gave them advice and knowledge.
- **You produced the magic wand** that saved them from…

So, how do you translate these into marketing messages? If you sell secure computer servers, you can hardly promise to make your client's life easier, however, you could say something like this:

"Our SuperSecureServer is resilient enough to withstand the most rigorous hacking attack, giving you complete confidence that no matter where you are, your information will remain safe and secure. What's more, our auto alert feature means you no longer have to provide a 24x7 watch-over service on your premises. Whoever is on call will receive an instant alert text which means that, out of hours, they can stay at home and only respond to incidents when they have to."

MAKE YOURSELF THE EXPERT

Common sense says you can't be an expert in everything, but you can – and should - be the expert in your field. It helps people to understand what you are selling.

Marketing is a huge field and we realised early on that we were being thought of in the same way as design companies, market research companies, marketing consultants and many other types of marketing companies. We needed to become experts, so we chose: B2B marketing.

And, within that niche, we specialise in providing a unique marketing coaching service that sets us apart from other companies in the sector, such as designers who might specialise in B2B marketing.

If people want help with their B2B marketing and want to improve their marketing skills or learn new ones, they know we are experts and that our coaching programmes will help them achieve their goals.

We make sure people know we are experts in the field by speaking regularly, producing books like this one and publishing articles that show we know what we are talking about.

Doctors instinctively know how to be experts. We trust them to give advice and believe whatever they tell us. They are the experts. Moreover, we would be referred to or seek out a specialist within the field of medicine for a particular problem - we wouldn't want a knee surgeon operating on our brain, would we?

Also, doctors don't have to find clients: patients approach them. When was the last time your doctor called you to find out if you had an ear infection and if she could offer you some antibiotic eardrops? You go to your doctor when you have a problem. Wouldn't it be great if you were seen as an expert in your field and people were beating a path to your door, wanting to make appointments to see you?

Where is your expertise?

What is your company really good at? How can you help clients and demonstrate that you know your stuff.

There are various ways to market your expertise, many of which are covered in *Chapter 3*, but, just for starters, think about the type of information that would help your clients do their jobs better. Can you produce a guide that showcases your knowledge and helps them, too? It could be a guide to surveying, which is related to digging holes - *Top Ten Things to Consider When Digging Foundations*.

Start being an expert and get people to come to you for advice. If you tell people you are an expert and can back it up, why wouldn't they believe you?

List all the possible areas where your expertise would be invaluable, then choose one that best suits your company, your products or services and will have a positive effect in helping you achieve the goals you identified at the beginning of this book.

You could be an expert on… why not write your ideas in the box over the page.

FIVE QUESTIONS YOU MUST BE ABLE TO ANSWER

Now that you are all fired up with new marketing messages that highlight your expertise and hook into the emotions of potential clients, you need to know how to communicate them effectively.

Keep it simple. Less is more.

Jack Trout, an expert on positioning and branding, has this to say about communication:

> *"The average mind is a dripping sponge… yet we continue to pour more information into the supersaturated sponge and are disappointed when our marketing messages fail to get through… "*

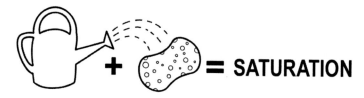 **= SATURATION**

In your enthusiasm to communicate how great your products and services are, it is easy to forget that people are bombarded with marketing messages, not just at work, but from the moment they wake up till they go to bed. Is it any wonder the last direct mail you sent out about all the amazing things you can do didn't seem to elicit a response?

When you start to write your next piece of marketing material, you must be able to answer the following questions.

1. Why should the prospect want to read what you have written?
2. Why should they believe what you have to say?
3. Why should they do anything about what you are offering?
4. Why should they act now?
5. What are the three key things you must communicate?

MAKING SOMETHING OUT OF NOTHING

Picture the scene: You are at a networking event or a seminar. You get talking to someone and the inevitable question arises:

"What do you do?"

You reply:

"I am a marketing consultant." or *"I run a marketing company."*

A real conversation stopper!

What about:

*"I'm Joanne Morley, the Marketing Success Coach.
I help businesses achieve their growth ambitions."*

They might laugh, or look at you strangely, but do you see the difference? It's all in the perception. A marketing consultant sounds boring, but a marketing success coach - what is that all about? They will probably wonder what it involves and will probe for more information.

So, what do you do? Write it down on the next page and, remember, it shouldn't be only you who knows about it - make sure everyone in the company can use it.

KEY MESSAGES – YOUR GUIDE TO COMMUNICATION SUCCESS

Once you know what you are actually selling and you have a list of the key phrases you want to use, it is time to develop a Key Messages Document that everyone in your company can use. This guide should be the basis for the development of your marketing communications, from emails to proposals and brochures. It can be used to ensure that you and your team don't find yourselves staring at a blank sheet of paper when writing copy or having to think about what to say to prospective clients.

The key messages should serve as a reference, ensuring that all communications are consistent and demonstrate the way in which you do business, highlighting your strengths and the benefits to potential customers.

The guide should include a range of statements that are not intended to be read as blocks of content but, rather, provide paragraphs and copy ideas to be used as a great foundation for producing:

- Brochure copy
- Website copy
- Letters and client communication
- Direct marketing
- Emails
- Press releases
- Proposals

You can use the information you gathered during your team session when you were working out what you were actually selling. In this way, you can use all those emotive words to help build up a better perception of your company.

The following are suggested headings and content for your Key Messages Document, taken from our own Key Messages Document.

Who Are You & What Do You Do?

These overview statements are designed to be used to describe your strengths and what you do. They can be used as a description on press releases or on the back of company brochures. They can also be used in conjunction with the other key messages in the guide to produce copy for proposals, client letters, etc.

> We are a proactive, experienced and motivational marketing company with the capability and focused expertise to help you unlock your marketing power. We work with you to transfer our marketing expertise so that you can realise your goals and have a positive impact on the growth of your company.

Key Message Statements

These are the key messages you need to communicate to your clients to let them know what you can do for them and how you can help them address their challenges. We suggest that you choose ten keywords and then develop paragraphs. Here is an example from Brighter Marketing:

Energy and enthusiasm

We have the focused energy and enthusiasm to motivate you towards marketing success. With creative workshops, innovative resources and action-orientated coaching, we will help you develop, then realise your marketing goals.

Your Values

Your values demonstrate how you do business, how you work with your clients and what is important to you and your clients. We suggest you choose around five values upon which you base your business. Here is an example from Brighter Marketing:

Honest and open

We work with you to learn what's important to your organisation, identifying key marketing issues and what you want to achieve. We will then provide honest and open recommendations about what we can accomplish working with you.

Why Should Clients Buy From You?

Determine the key reasons individuals should want to buy from you and work out how you can provide solutions to their challenges. We recommend that you develop between five and ten reasons, using a keyword to develop a paragraph or bullet points. Here is a Brighter Marketing example:

Marketing inspiration

At Brighter Marketing we are committed to inspiring great marketing and creating an enthusiasm for marketing that increases confidence, motivation and, ultimately, the performance of the organisation.

Your Hot Buttons

Hot buttons are the short, sharp sentences that tell potential clients what you can do for them. Use sentences that start with increase, save, gain, enhance, improve and reduce, or similar active words. A couple of examples from Brighter Marketing:

We can increase your marketing confidence and motivation to deliver improved strategies that will deliver marketing effectiveness.

Save time and resources by working with a marketing partner who can take your marketing to the next level with one-to-one coaching and guidance.

Words That Matter

These are the keywords you use to describe your company and the way you work. They act as building blocks for producing copy and provide the words you use to communicate with your clients and potential clients.

Some examples from Brighter Marketing:

WE ARE...				
Committed	Enthusiastic	Intelligent	Approachable	Challenging
Fun	Experts	Realistic	Practical	Loyal
Proactive	Open	Honest	Purposeful	Considerate
Understanding	Helpful	Straightforward	Organised	Adaptive
Imaginative	Creative	Decisive	Strong	Dedicated

WHAT DO OUR CLIENTS WANT FROM US?				
Magic wand	Perspective	Companionship	Support	Experience
Wisdom	Attention	Understanding	For us to value them	For us to help them
Motivation	Partnership	Control	Insight	Trust
Appreciation	Knowledge	For us to listen	Success	Improvement

KEYWORDS				
Relevant	Quality	Simple	Effective	Explore
Dedication	Energy	Intensity	Ability	Capacity
Capability	Influence	Powerful	Flexible	Happy
Durable	Confident	Easy to work with	Focused	Discover

EMOTIVE MARKETING WORDS

There are three great books that are full of powerful marketing words you can use in your marketing copy. They do include words and phrases that are appropriate to consumer marketing. However, they are also useful in B2B marketing and can be a great help when you want to write a strong call to action or are seeking another word for "free".

'Phrases That Sell: The Ultimate Phrase Finder to Help You Promote Your Products, Services and Ideas' by Edward W. Werz and Sally Germain

'Words that Sell: More Than 6,000 Entries to Help You Promote Your Products, Services and Ideas' by Richard Bayan

'More Words that Sell' by Richard Bayan

If you are looking for emotive words to get you started; words that will help you in your marketing campaigns and get people to take action, look at these power words, words that will get attention:

Absolutely	Amazing	Approved	Authentic	Complete
Endorsed	Excellent	Exciting	Exclusive	Expert
Fascinating	Genuine	Guaranteed	Helpful	Immediately
Improved	Informative	Instructive	Interesting	Limited
Noted	Outstanding	Personalised	Popular	Powerful
Practical	Professional	Profitable	Proven	Quality
Quickly	Rare	Reduced	Remarkable	Reliable
Reveal	Secrets	Security	Selected	Simplified
Special	Successful	Superior	Tested	Unique
Unparalleled	Unusual	Useful	Valuable	Wonderful

Here are some phrases that urge your customer to take action:

Act now!	An incredible offer
Be the first to qualify for	A unique opportunity to
Free guide that explains…	Experience the power of
Get facts that will help you to…	Four easy ways to register
Get your copy of our guide NOW!	Simply call us
Be sure and book your place on our…	Take action today
Reply today to reserve your copy…	What are you waiting for?
Stocks are limited…	Be one of the first to experience
Don't delay…	Try it
Now available	Sign up for our guide to…

There are hundreds more words and phrases you can use to make your marketing copy more emotive and interesting and, more importantly, drive your clients to take action. Remember, don't sell the product or service, sell what it will do for them and keep it short, simple and to the point.

4. How To Find Profitable Clients

"Nothing can add more power to your life than concentrating all your energies on a limited set of targets."
NIDO QUBEIN

Here's a true story…

One Christmas, the managing director of a very large company received a direct mail piece. We haven't used the original, but the following conveys the essence of the piece. It was printed on very thin A4 paper, folded and sent in a small envelope, addressed in person, with "private and confidential" written on the envelope.

Special Offer!

BUY one of our Hexal filing cabinets before 17th December and you will receive a **FREE tin of luxury biscuits!**

Call Sue on 01111 222666 To place your order today!

There were many things wrong with the flyer, such as the quality of the paper, and the messaging could have been much better. However, the main problem was the person they sent it to.

The company does buy a large amount of office furniture, but it is definitely not the managing director's responsibility and, even if it was, the quality of the piece and the offer of free biscuits certainly wouldn't have enticed her to "call Sue" and buy. What's more marking the envelope "private and confidential" when it contained marketing information was also a big mistake. There was nothing confidential inside and it could have been opened by her PA.

They might have had more success if they had sent it to the office manager who was actually responsible for buying office furniture and who might just have wanted a free tin of biscuits for Christmas!

TARGET LIKE A LASER BEAM

Defining who you are selling to is critical to the success of B2B marketing. And it's not just about identifying the companies that would want to buy your products and services - you must identify the decision-makers who have the power to buy.

There is little point in creating powerful marketing messages that are then used on marketing campaigns that are sent out to individuals who don't have responsibility for buying what you are selling. No matter how great your marketing campaign looks, the response will be poor if you don't direct it at the right people.

YOUR IDEAL CLIENT

The first stage in defining your target audience is to develop criteria for the type of companies that would be interested in buying your products or services.

To start with, write a description of your ideal client. It could be based on the clients you already have or ones you want to work with.

The characteristics of my ideal client are:

Then write a description of the worst client.

The characteristics of my worst client are:

We undertake this exercise because many of our clients argue that they will work with any type of company. However, when we get them to do this exercise, they begin to see that there are definitely clients who are not good business for them and that if they focused their efforts on those who are, the results of their marketing would improve.

Now you know the characteristics of the clients you want to work with, you need to define them so that you can be clear about the type of companies and decision-makers you want to target.

The following can be useful as a checklist to help you segment the market and focus your efforts. You don't have to choose a segment from each of the options, but you should, at the very least, choose two to define your target audience.

VERTICAL SECTOR
Is there a particular vertical sector you can target? For example, is your software only relevant to financial services companies?

NUMBER OF EMPLOYEES
Does there have to be a certain number of employees in the organisation? Do you sell your product only to companies with 200+ employees, or would smaller businesses buy it?

TURNOVER
Is turnover important? Does the company have to turn over at least £10m because of the cost or scope of the service that you offer?

GEOGRAPHICAL AREA
Can you only service a certain geographical area? There is little point in targeting companies in an area where you can't provide your product or service.

SPECIFIC INFORMATION
In some cases, you may want to drill further down, such as to the type of computers they have on site, or the number of servers, if you work in the IT field. Or it may be that you need to know they have a certain type of printing press installed as you service these types of printers.

If you sell high-end IT security products, you might have a list that looks something like the one below. Of course, yours might be more detailed, and the more you can weed out those companies that are not relevant to you, the more effective your marketing will be.

VERTICAL SECTOR
None, work with all companies – sector not important

NUMBER OF EMPLOYEES
Must be over 250 employees

TURNOVER
Turnover £10m at least – due to cost of investment

GEOGRAPHICAL AREA
We can work in UK

SPECIFIC INFORMATION
At least 10 servers and a multi site network

This is great. You now know the type of companies you are targeting, but who actually does the buying? As demonstrated in the example at the beginning of this chapter, it is absolutely vital that you get through to the decision-maker. The next section helps you to confirm that you know exactly who to target with your marketing messages.

THE DECISION-MAKER SEALS THE DEAL

People buy from people. You're not marketing to companies; you're marketing to living, breathing human beings who have the decision-making power to choose to buy from you. Therefore, the most important part of targeting your marketing efforts is finding the people who can actually make a decision to buy from you.

In some cases, it is easy to identify the decision-maker. For example, if you are selling IT products, it is likely to be one or a combination of the following:

- IT Manager
- IT Director
- Network Manager
- Telecoms Manager
- Chief information Officer
- Chief Technical Officer

However, if you are in a different sort of business, such as a security company that provides a manned guarding service, you might need to dig deeper. You might need to think more laterally about the type of decision-makers you want to contact and who they are.

You might draw up a list that includes:

- Facilities Manager
- Operations Manager
- Operations Director
- Owner or Managing Director
- Security Manager
- PA or secretary to Managing Director
- Stores Manager
- Site Manager

As you can see, there is a range of job titles whose holders may or may not be responsible for buying security. So, you will have to do some research and match the job titles to the type of company. For example, if, on your list of target companies, the company size is 50 employees and over, you can assume there probably won't be a Security Manager and your target is more likely to be the Owner or Managing Director. For larger companies, there will probably be a Facilities Manager or Security Manager.

In some cases, the only sure-fire way to find out who is responsible for buying your product or service is to call up and ask. They may or may not give you the person's name, but at least you will find out their job title and can begin to build an intelligent list of key decision-makers.

FINDING YOUR IDEAL CLIENTS – BUYING DATA

Once you have identified your target companies and the decision-makers within them, you need names if your marketing is to be really successful. Where do you get this information?

The easiest way is to buy a list of names and contact details that match your targeted list from a database or list company. Be warned, though: use a reputable company that is, at the very least, a member of the Direct Marketing Association (in the UK) and guarantees that its lists are up-to-date and relevant. Don't risk buying out-of-date names and contact details.

Working with a reputable list provider is particularly important when buying email names and addresses. It is your duty to check that the individuals have opted in to receive information via email.

Where do you find these lists? There are various places, including two general companies we have worked with and found to be reputable:

Marketing File (*www.marketingfile.com*)

An established and reputable broker for a range of list companies. Choose from general lists through to more targeted lists such as Marketing Decision-Makers. You can input your target criteria online and they will produce a count of the number of businesses that match your needs. They will also provide five test names and contact details to enable you to check the quality of the list.

Electric Marketing (*www.electricmarketing.co.uk*)

A smaller list broker, but still with a good range of lists for the UK that enable you to focus on specific areas.

For more specific data, there are companies that specialise in particular areas. Here are a few you might find useful:

Laing & Buisson (*www.laingbuisson.co.uk*) and Binleys (*www.binleys.com*)

Both specialise in the healthcare sector. Binleys focuses on the NHS and Laing & Buisson on care homes and the private sector.

The Manufacturing Database
(*www.themanufacturer.com*)

Specialists in providing decision-makers in the manufacturing industry.

VNU One-to-One (*www.vnuone-to-one.co.uk*)

Their lists cover IT as well as financial decision-makers in the UK and Europe. They publish Computing magazine and financial publications and provide targeted lists based on their subscription lists.

Mardev (*www.mardev.com*)

They provide access to a wide range of specialist marketing lists from Asian food to telecoms, as they are a worldwide publishing company with access to wide range of subscription lists.

The key to marketing success is to find your target market and to focus on it. It is always better to send out 20 targeted direct mail pieces than to send 2,000 to an untargeted list. As with your marketing messages, less is more, so before you send out your next direct mail campaign, stop and think. Each frank or stamp costs money - is the person you are sending it to in the right company for your business and, more importantly, are you sending it to the right person?

5. Creativity

"I am neither especially clever, nor am I especially gifted. I am only very, very curious."
ALBERT EINSTEIN

Many theory-based marketing books often don't mention that, for marketing to be successful, there has to an element of creativity. If you ask people if they are creative, a high percentage will say "no". But that's not true: we can all be creative. All we need is the right attitude and the tools to get going.

In companies all over the world, creativity is usually limited to brainstorming sessions. These sessions, although valuable, often don't produce any creative results because of the way they are structured. The gem of a good idea can be ruined because another person says "it would never work".

If you have gone to the effort of developing power marketing messages and finding the right target market, you must make the way you communicate with them stand out from the crowd.

If you want to get really creative, there is a great book you can use to get your creative juices flowing: *Thinker Toys* by Michael Michalko, which contains a range of creative thinking exercises and tools.

To get you started, here are a couple overleaf that you might want to use.

FIND YOUR MARKETING GAP

Use this exercise if you are struggling to differentiate yourself or are looking for a niche within your particular industry. We used this tool to find our niche. It is really simple.

Take a piece of paper and draw four boxes, as in the illustration below. Then find two attributes or niches that fit the industry in which you operate. Using Brighter Marketing as an example, on our first matrix we chose the following:

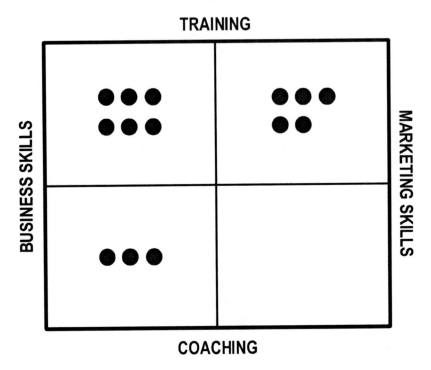

TRAINING

BUSINESS SKILLS / **MARKETING SKILLS**

COACHING

We realised that although there were lots of companies providing business skills training as well as business coaching programmes for executives, there didn't seem to be anyone offering marketing skills coaching. This wasn't the first matrix we came up with; we tried different ones until we spotted a gap in the market.

We were specialists in marketing, but the competition in marketing training was tough and we didn't want to be just another marketing training company. The matrix approach helped us to see that if we combined coaching and marketing skills, we could provide a different kind of service, and one that didn't infringe on executive business coaching either.

Draw some matrices and keep looking at different attributes and types of industry until you hit on a gap or niche that might just give you the edge over your competitors.

CREATE NEW IDEAS FROM WHAT YOU ALREADY HAVE

This is a tool credited to Dr Fritz Zwicky. It can be very useful in a variety of situations, to find new products or, in the example we have used from the *Thinker Toys* book, to find a new way of marketing a book.

The premise is simple: you take what you already have and create an ideas box that can produce even more ideas. The example provided, shows the generation of new ideas for the marketing of an old book of standard speeches that had a really bad sales record. The publisher wanted to sell it but it just wasn't shifting.

The first thing you need to do is to decide on four attributes that will affect the marketing of the book. In the example, provided the following were chosen; packaging, distribution, promotion and selling. The second step is to develop a grid that uses these four attributes at the top of the grid. You then think of all the different ways you could develop each of these attributes and list them underneath. There are ten given in the example but you can have as many or as few as you like.

The grid opposite shows how it works, and the highlighted boxes show how they developed a new product from those 4 key areas.

IDEA BOX: MARKETING A BOOK

	PACKAGING	DISTRIBUTION	PROMOTION	SELLING
1	Cover: hard or soft	Traditional distributors & wholesalers	Advertising	Direct Sales Force
2	USB stick	Distribute with other publishers	Book Reviews	Direct Mail
3	Package with other items	Distribute at exhibitions & trade fairs	Talk shows	Special sales premium & incentives
4	Package to adapt to seasonality	Computer stores	Bonus inserts & coupons	Telemarketing
5	Gift Item	Other book stores	Videos based on the book	Door-to-door
6	Solo or series	Supermarkets	Tie-in with charity	Independent reps
7	Package interestingly	Direct to consumer	Free articles in newspapers	Sell to schools & libraries
8	Package with built-in gimmick	Through manufacturer of related products	Seminars & workshops	Sales kits
9	Creative package	Self-publish	Time discounts	Author connections
10	Online – generator	Through home parties	Contest or competition	Sell foreign rights

From this grid, the publisher came up with the idea of packaging the speeches as scrolls in cardboard "cans" and to call them Canned Speeches. This new product was sold by the direct sales force into office supply stores as well as to standard retail outlets. The publisher wrote and submitted articles to major newspapers about this novel package, earning some free publicity.

You can't fail to be creative using this method, so see what new products and marketing activities you could create.

6. Beyond The Logo… Making Your Brand Work For You

"What's a brand? A singular idea or concept that you own inside the mind of the prospect."
AL RIES – 22 IMMUTABLE LAWS OF BRANDING

What your organisation means to your clients is much more than the logo and set of associated images you use to represent the products and services you sell. It's about everything you do that connects in any way with the client.

Think about it. You could have the most expertly designed logo that transcends all media and wins design awards, but it won't mean a thing if the clients who buy from you associate it with bad service or faulty products. Your brand should communicate your values, your beliefs and the real personality of your organisation, so that, no matter which angle your organisation, products and services are viewed from, they provide a consistent message to the client.

To start with, here is a simple checklist to use to make sure the physical representation of your brand (your logo) can be used on everything you do:

- ✓ It should be simple and easy to recognise for use on all media, from a website to printed brochures.
- ✓ You should have several versions of the logo in different file formats such as JPG, EPS, etc, for use in different media.
- ✓ The logo must work in black and white and greyscale. You may not always be able to use your logo in colour, or be in control of how it is printed out, e.g., on a mono laser printer.
- ✓ The logo should be scalable and identifiable at both large and small scale - it should still be recognisable it if it was used on a pen or on a billboard.
- ✓ Any fonts used should be inexpensive and easily readable.

44

If you are thinking of creating a new brand or want to update an existing brand, use the following template to brief a designer:

Describe your business and the products and services you provide

What is the vision for the company?

Who is your target audience – who are you selling to?

What words would you use to describe the values your company has?

What do you want your target audience to think about your company?

Who are your competitors? Include websites.

What do you want the brand to look like?

Are there any specific branding requirements?

Any other comments?

YOUR SHOP FRONT

Imagine a client found your company via the back door, via a route other than the normal sales channels?

- Would your stockroom look as impressive and tidy as your shop front?
- Would the people working there be courteous and helpful?
- How would the employees speak about your organisation?
- Would the client recognise your organisation? Would there be a disconnection between what they knew about you and what they found in the stock room?

This shop analogy is a useful one to think about, regardless of what your organisation does. It demonstrates that although it is important to develop and present a positive image to your clients and potential clients through consistent branding on your website, company literature, etc, there are other factors to consider. This includes the way employees speak, the way they dress, the state of your offices or distribution centres - they all have an impact on the perception of your brand.

WHERE IS YOUR BRAND?

Regardless of the size of your organisation, spending time on your brand – not just your logo – will pay dividends. Answering the following questions will help you form a clear picture of where your brand is now and where, ultimately, you want it to be.

Think long and hard about what your organisation does. You may think you just sell widgets to the powerboat industry but, when you really think about it, you do much more, don't you? Perhaps you:

- Save your clients time because your widgets can be assembled quickly.
- Reduce their costs because your widgets are made out of a cost-effective steel alloy.
- Enable them to manufacture the fastest speedboats in the industry because your widget is an essential part of the engine.

No matter what you do, really think about what your product or service means to the client. This will help you understand what your brand represents to them. You could discover that, to them, you are much more than a widget supplier and that you are, in fact, integral to the success of their organisation.

DOES YOUR LOGO WORK?

Although your logo is not your company brand, it is important to ensure that you have a logo and associated imagery that is used consistently across your literature, from your letterhead to your employees' uniforms. Ask yourself:

- Are you proud of your logo and company image? Does it work for or against you? Has the company moved on but your logo stayed the same?
- Is the logo and company image used consistently throughout the organisation? For example, is the logo that is used on the website the same as the one used on marketing literature?
- If it is used electronically, is it of a good quality?
- Can your logo be used in colour, greyscale and black and white?
- Can it scale easily from a badge to an exhibition stand and still be recognisable?
- Is it memorable?

If you answered 'no' to any of these questions, think about what your logo says about your organisation and what you do. If it isn't doing the job, act now - you should be proud of how your company looks to potential clients.

WHAT DO YOU LOOK LIKE?

You may think this is all about your logo - it isn't. It means: What does your organisation look like to your clients. What perception do they form of your company through visiting your offices or interacting with your employees?

Have you mystery-shopped your own company recently? Try it and see what views you form. Sample questions you could ask yourself include:

- How do employees interact with clients?
- How are the employees dressed when they meet clients?
- How are the phones answered and queries dealt with?
- What do the offices or factory look like? Are they appealing and what impression do they give to potential clients?
- How are clients greeted when they visit your offices?
- What do employees look like? Are they bright, happy, etc? There aren't many organisations with unhappy employees and happy clients.
- Is the promotion of the brand omnipresent throughout the organisation?

WHAT IS YOUR PERSONALITY?

All brands have a personality. It may be that you are associated with quality or that when clients see your logo they think of the integrity of your sales force. Think about people with strong personalities and how easily you are drawn towards them. Think about friends you have known for years and those who have come and gone. Why are you still friends with some and not others? They probably have qualities you identify with and appreciate, such as not letting you down in times of need or they are fun to be around.

This doesn't change just because a personality is encapsulated within an organisation. By striving to be friendly, open and honest, your company will attract clients and make them feel good about choosing you. Think about your brand's personality:

- Do you make it easy for clients to do business with you?
- What does your brand stand for? Innovation, creativity, quality, integrity, etc?
- What do people think when they see your brand?
- What are the key attributes that will attract potential clients to your organisation and, secondly, maintain their loyalty?
- What personality do you want your organisation to have that connects with your target audience and draws them to you?

Think of all the words that describe your brand's personality and use them in your marketing literature, on your website and in the way your employees speak to clients. By understanding and building your brand, you can start to connect with your target audience. After all, people buy from people and if they can identify with your organisation, you are halfway there.

WEAR THE CLIENT'S SHOES

Working in your organisation can give you a clouded view of what your brand represents to clients. You make assumptions about what clients want or need and what they think about your organisation. Some of the largest companies in the world have had their market share eroded because they didn't wear the client's shoes once in a while and experience the brand for themselves. If you haven't done one of our exercises in *Chapter 3* about thinking like your client, this is a good time to do so.

Mystery shopping companies exist for a reason and they can often provide some powerful intelligence on how your brand is perceived in the marketplace. Even if you don't use them, try being a client for a day. This can reveal some important things about your brand and the way you work with clients.

WHAT HAPPENS INSIDE?

We have touched on what happens inside your organisation and how this can reflect on the brand as a whole. The look and feel of a great brand can be completely eroded by bad client service or faulty products. Consider how your brand is promoted internally.

The most successful companies are focused on promoting the brand to their employees and encourage them to reflect it in all aspects of their work. Whether they are answering telephones or are at the forefront of the sales force, they are representing your brand and should have a clear idea of what it represents for the clients.

The internal marketing of your brand should not be forgotten. If employees don't know what the brand stands for, how you can expect them to promote it at all times? It is important that your organisational culture reflects your brand personality and values.

- Communicate the brand and its value at every opportunity. This could be through internal newsletters, monthly meetings or through awards for excellence.

- Don't force the brand on to your employees. Work the brand and its values into all aspects of working life, from their uniforms to the training they undertake for client service. By drip-feeding rather than force-feeding, they can move from unconscious incompetence to unconscious competence over time.

Clients don't just see a brand on its own: their mind is unconsciously processing a range of feelings, emotions and experiences to form a perception of your organisation. Consistency of message, logo and values are key to making all the elements of your brand work together to form a positive and cohesive brand.

A FINAL THOUGHT...

This is a classic story that clearly demonstrates how the brand is more than just a logo and how easily it can be eroded overnight.

April 1991 – Annual Convention of the Institute of Directors

Gerald Ratner, the Managing Director of well known UK high street jewellers Ratner's, gave a presentation on the cost-effectiveness of his products, including a pair of earrings:

"People say, how can you sell these earrings for such a low price? I say, because it's total crap. We even sell a pair of earrings for under £1, which is cheaper than a prawn sandwich from Marks & Spencer, but I have to say the earrings probably won't last as long."

These comments heralded the demise of Ratner's. Its brand was effectively demolished overnight. Before Mr Ratner made his comments, shares were trading at 189p. Within eight months they had dropped to 27p; down 86%. Eventually, Mr Ratner was forced to resign.

Ratner's logo looked great, their shop assistants were friendly and, although they weren't Tiffany & Co, the general public associated them with quality, affordable jewellery. The whole brand had been eroded by two simple statements, yet they looked the same, their employees acted the same and their shop fronts hadn't changed. What had changed was people's perception, and this led to their ultimate demise.

If you want to read more about brands and positioning your company, here are two great books to give you lots of useful information:

- *22 Immutable Laws of Branding* – Al and Laura Ries
- *Positioning: The Battle For Your Mind* – Al Ries and Jack Trout

7. Ways To Create Marketing Magnetism

"Marketing is too important to be left to the marketing department."
DAVID PACKARD

Imagine you had a strong magnet primed with your marketing messages and all you had to do was point it at your target audience and they would be drawn to you, like a piece of metal would be drawn to a magnet.

Wouldn't that be amazing? Every time you wanted new clients or to keep existing clients close to you, you would just get out the marketing magnet and, hey presto! There they were.

Let us tell you a secret: you can create marketing magnetism. It's not difficult - you just have to open your mind to how marketing really works, and choose the tactics that best suit your needs.

Also, we know that marketing is not just about attracting new clients: you must have marketing activities that keep existing clients loyal. After all, according to Pareto's Law, 20% of your customers will be providing 80% of your profits, so it is also important to take care of what you already have. *Chapter 9* looks at some of the ways you can market to existing and lapsed clients.

Before we get started, a brief word of warning. If this was the first chapter you turned to, great! We know you are eager to get started. However, it is worth reading *Chapter 2* first, to confirm that you have a vision of what you want your marketing to achieve.

One last thing: reading our book is a great thing to do. We want you to succeed, create great marketing campaigns and increase revenues.

However, we know from experience that reading doesn't always translate into action.

"You see in life, lots of people know what to do, they read and listen to books and other people, but few people actually do what they know or find out. Knowing is NOT enough! You must take action."
ANTHONY ROBBINS

For any marketing to be effective, you must take action.

MARKETING WITHOUT SPENDING A PENNY

First, some marketing activities that will cost you nothing, except time and maybe a bit of effort. If you want your marketing to be highly successful, you will have to part with some money at some point, but let's get started with things you can do immediately.

You probably already know about some of these methods. But are you doing them? And, if you are, are you doing them to their full potential? Choose two or three activities you want to start doing or to do better. Be honest with yourself.

Networking

You probably attend networking events from time to time, or go to industry events and exhibitions. But do you really get anything out of these occasions? Do you actually meet any potential clients? If you take just a little time and follow our simple formula, you will begin to notice a difference.

Attend Relevant Events. Go only to events that are likely to be attended by your target audience. If your target audience is small to medium businesses, don't waste your time attending FTSE 250 events. You won't meet the decision-makers you need to target.

Business Cards. Networking is not about dishing out your business card to as many people as possible and then leaving. Ask the organisers who will be attending the event; get a list so you can pinpoint the people you would like to meet. Or ask the organisers in advance if you can sit on a table with the people you want to meet.

Networking is Not Selling. Once you know who you want to target at the event, just find them and have a chat with them. There is no need for a hard sell, just introduce yourself and listen to them and what they have to say. It is much more beneficial to find out about them, than to talk about yourself and your company. You never know what you might find out or who they might know. So, keep your mouth shut for the first few minutes and actively listen.

Finding Partners. Networking is an ideal way to find companies that could be potential network or referral partners. For example, we have met many referral partners such as banks, solicitors and HR consultants who we are happy to refer and vice-versa. It's not about getting referrals on the day, but about arranging to meet later to find out how you could be of mutual benefit.

Get Some Training. If you feel nervous about networking, get some help. There are plenty of training courses that teach the basic skills you need to be an effective networker. To begin with, you can always attend with a colleague who is used to networking, but, over time, you must get used to going it alone.

Follow-up. If you meet someone you think could be a potential client or referral partner, send them an email or call them after the event to arrange to meet. This is a crucial element of networking and is key to developing relationships. However, this doesn't mean getting the list of attendees from the organisers and sending out a blanket email; only follow up with the people you actually meet.

Be Brave. What's the worst that can happen? At least 50% of the attendees will be feeling just like you and would be extremely happy if you just went up to them and talked to them as they stood there alone with their back against the wall.

Be Generous. In his book *Love is the Killer App: How to Win Business and Influence Friends*, Tim Sanders points out that by being generous with your expertise, knowledge and contacts, you benefit more than if you hold back information and don't share. The theory is that the more you give, the more you get back. And, as the well respected Chief Solutions

Officer at Yahoo, Tim says: "Everyone in your address book is a potential partner for every person you meet, everyone can fit somewhere in your ever-expanding business universe."

Referrals

Referrals are one of the most effective marketing tools and getting them costs nothing. There are two types of referrals: those that come from existing clients and those that come from your referral network. Let's take a look at each.

Just to clarify, by referral we mean a real introduction. This is where your client or referral partner calls the prospect, tells them about you and your services and prepares them for a phone call or email from you. It's not just a contact name they pass on to you, that is almost the same as making a cold call.

Referrals from existing clients. How often do you ask your existing clients for referrals? Your clients can be one of the best aids to create marketing magnetism; all you have to do is ask. Once you have established a good working relationship and they know you are delivering a good service, pick up the phone or take them out for lunch to discuss the working relationship. During the course of the conversation, ask them if they know two other companies they would be happy to introduce to you, based on the great work you have been doing for them. We find most clients are happy to do this and can usually think of two companies immediately.

Referrals from your network. Your referral network should consist of around five partners who properly understand your business and the type of clients you are targeting. You need to spend time with them so that they really understand your range of services and you understand theirs. It is difficult to have more than five as you must maintain good relationships with them and meet regularly. The introductions they make must be right for your business. For example, if our referral partners didn't really understand what we do, they could introduce us to companies that are looking for design services, not coaching.

Speaking

One great way of putting yourself in front of an audience of potential clients is to identify and take up speaking opportunities. From your local Chamber of Commerce and special interest groups to speaking slots at exhibitions, opportunities abound. However, you must talk about industry matters, or give a talk on marketing or whatever your expert subject is. This is not a sales presentation; give the audience some useful information and, if appropriate, at the end let them know who you are and the type of services you provide.

Speaking at events also helps you to develop your expert profile, so that potential clients know you are knowledgeable about your subject matter and that you could potentially help them with a particular problem or challenge.

Re-marketing

You need to be creative, but think of ways you can re-market the products and services you already have into a more attractive package. For example, if you provide a service, can you develop different service levels - Silver, Gold and Platinum - so that you can differentiate between them and give your clients a choice? In Robert Cialdini's book *YES! 50 Secrets from the Science of Persuasion*, he says that offering three versions of a product or service can pay dividends.

When buyers have a choice of two products or services in a range, they usually compromise by opting for the cheapest version. However, if a third product is introduced which is more expensive than the other two, people will generally move from choosing the lowest-cost product to the mid-priced one.

By simply re-marketing your products or services, you could see revenue increase as customers select the mid-priced option, rather than the cheaper of the two options you are currently providing.

Your Clients

Your clients are a free marketing tool, not only because they can refer you, but because they can provide real-life confirmation that you do what you say you do. Working with them to develop testimonials or case studies based on the work you have done with them can be extremely rewarding. We have outlined the type of questions you need to ask to get the most out of the phone call or interview you have with them. We'll cover case studies in more detail later in this chapter.

Case study checklist:

- ☐ What does your company do - can you provide a company profile?
- ☐ What were the challenges you faced before working with us?
- ☐ What goals did you want to achieve?
- ☐ Why did you choose to work with us?
- ☐ How did our services/products/technology enable you to achieve your goals?
- ☐ What difference has the service/product/technology made to your business? What can you do now that you couldn't before?
- ☐ What would you say was the best thing about working with us?

Once you have this information, you can write a case study or testimonial that you can include on your website, print out to include in proposals or to take along to sales meetings.

Your Knowledge

Knowledge is one of the most under-used marketing tools. If you are an expert in your subject, don't hold back - give people the information they need to solve their biggest challenges. If you have a product or service, lead with information about solving problems, not information about the product or service itself.

A mistake many people make is to hold on to their knowledge, to keep it back for when the sale is made. By then, it can be too late. We don't advocate giving away everything you know, just enough to demonstrate you know what you are talking about and can help someone begin to solve problems and meet challenges. It helps to build trust and shows you are willing to share knowledge early in the business relationship. In fact, in many cases, providing a potential client with an informative guide can be much more effective than leaving behind your company brochure.

A guide says much more about your competencies than a glossy brochure ever can. And one of the easiest ways to do this, is to write a guide or "white paper" for clients and potential clients on a subject you know inside out. It is important to write it with them in mind and that it relates to something specific, contains valuable information and has an interesting title.

Example guide titles:

- How to Generate Sales Leads Through Internet Marketing
- Top Ten Ways to Secure Your IT Network
- Insider Tips on Developing Business Property
- 20 Ways to Increase Profitability
- The IR 35 Rule Explained Simply and Easily
- 100 Tips for Stressed-out IT Managers
- How to Create Successful Direct Mail Campaigns
- Manual Handling – The Definitive Guide
- 87 Ways to Improve Your Sales Performance
- Six Steps to Six-Figure Profits
- Everything You Didn't Know About Firewalls
- Manager's Guide to Listening Skills
- Little Known Ways to Develop Your Sales Pipeline
- Everything You Need to Know About IP Address Management

Choose a title that will interest your target market and get writing. It doesn't have to be expertly designed, but it does have to be easy to read, have clear images and diagrams to explain concepts and provide the reader with genuinely useful information. Then all you have to do is publish it to a PDF and start using it. There are lots of ways you can use it - here are a few:

- Put it on your website for download – you can ask for people's details if you want to know who is downloading it.
- Use it as a hook in a direct mail – "Contact us for your FREE Guide to…"
- Distribute it to attendees at your next speaking engagement as a thank you for attending the event.
- Take copies to your next exhibition or seminar and give to delegates who show an interest.
- Send to prospective clients instead of the usual brochure, via email as a PDF or in the post as a print-out.

STOP AND THINK BEFORE PARTING WITH YOUR CASH

Before undertaking any marketing activity that you have to pay for, no matter how large your marketing budget, stop and think. It is important to spend any budget you have with care and focus.

Even when we were marketing managers and had the luxury of large marketing budgets, we always stopped and considered whether the activity we were undertaking would help us achieve our marketing objectives and the company goals. And what's more we always made sure we were getting value for money. That didn't mean always going with the cheapest provider - it meant that we worked only with agencies that understood our needs and, more importantly, could help us achieve our targets.

Don't waste your marketing budget on activities that simply aren't going to get you where you want to be.

GET CREATIVE – GUERRILLA TACTICS

This book covers the main marketing activities - direct mail, seminars, etc - that are successfully used by companies all over the world. Although these can be incredibly powerful ways of marketing your company, sometimes you need to be more creative and think of ways to reach your target decision-makers with marketing tactics that often don't cost very much but will grab their attention.

The term "guerrilla marketing" was coined by Jay Conrad Levinson in his 1984 book of the same name. He had developed an unconventional and low-budget approach to marketing that relied on imagination, time and effort, rather than big bucks. The ideas were mainly for small and medium-sized companies. It is worth reading his revised edition, although some UK and European readers may find some of his tactics a little aggressive.

Here are some examples of guerrilla marketing tactics we or our clients have used.

Temp Recruitment Company

On a Monday morning, they sent fresh cream cakes by courier to clients they hadn't heard from in a while, with a message saying:

"We know you are busy, but take
a break and enjoy the cake."

They then called the client to confirm they had received the cakes, to find out if there was any reason they hadn't been in touch recently and to see if they needed any temps that month. When the clients took the call, in most case they were eating or had eaten the cakes and were in a great frame of mind to agree to meet the company to review their temporary staff arrangements!

Catering Company

A new catering company wanted to attract some corporate clients. They wanted potential clients to sample their amazing food, not just see pictures and read menus. So they targeted office buildings in the city centre and visited them just before lunch with their gourmet food attractively packaged and branded.

They knew getting the food to the decision-maker wouldn't be easy, so initially they befriended the receptionist and gave her samples to try. With the receptionist as their ally, they were able to take in more samples which the receptionist was happy to take to the person responsible for booking corporate buffets and to supply that person's name to the catering company.

Guess what - next time the firm's regular catering company couldn't handle an order, this company got the call.

DIRECT MAIL – SEVEN STEPS TO SUCCESS

It is a sad fact that most direct mail ends up in the bin, usually because of a combination of the following:

- It is sent to the wrong company, one not in your target market
- It is sent to the right company, but not to the decision-maker
- It is a plain sales letter and doesn't stand out
- It is a well designed direct mail but the main message is not compelling
- There is no call to action - the recipient is not asked to do anything as a result of receiving it
- It is boring and full of product or service descriptions
- The quality of the paper and print is poor
- There is no creativity, it doesn't stand out

So, is there any point in using direct mail as a marketing tool, since it is likely to end up in the bin? The answer is yes - it is only most direct mail that ends up in the bin, not all. Follow our simple Seven-step system, to help give your direct mail an extra boost.

Step 1 – Your Intention

Before designing or writing your direct mail, decide what you want to achieve by sending it out - this provides the direction for the direct mail. A recipient is unlikely to pick up the phone and place a large order with you as a result of a direct mail. What you want them to do is respond and be interested in your products and services. Here are some suggestions for what you may want to achieve:

- Sign up to free 30-day trial of your product
- Claim free guide, book or "white paper"
- Earn money off or percentage discount on first order
- A book valued at £25 free to the first 25 respondents
- Attendance at a seminar or workshop
- Claim a discount voucher

Write down what you want to achieve with your direct mail:

Step 2 – Your Target Audience

As outlined in *Chapter 4*, you must have a clear picture of your target market. You must ensure every direct mail piece you send goes to the decision-maker in the type of company you have established as being an ideal client.

Having identified your target market and the number of individuals you wish to mail, you will have to decide whether to send the direct mail in one hit or in stages. This will depend on your resources. If you have identified 5,000 individuals in your target market, sending to all of them at the same time could make it difficult for you to follow them up if you get a good response.

You should expect a response rate of between 2 and 7% to a business-to-business direct mail. If you mail 5,000 people and an average of 4% respond, you will have 200 sales leads to follow up. This sounds fantastic, but if you are a small company, can you handle 200 hot leads?

Also, it doesn't allow you to follow up the people who didn't respond (Step 7). We usually recommend sending direct mail out in small batches so that you can manage the response efficiently. If you send a limited amount every couple of weeks, you will have time to send the information recipients request, then call them to find out if you can be of further help. This stop-start method keeps you in control, enabling you to make the most of every enquiry.

However, there is an exception to this rule. If you are using direct mail to encourage people to attend a seminar you are running or an exhibition you are attending, you will need to ensure that everyone receives the direct mail well ahead of the event.

Write down your target market, how many people are on your list and how many direct mails you are going to send out per week.

Step 3 – The Headline Message, The Hook

You will need a headline message and a hook to generate interest from your target audience. Refer back to *Chapter 3* for ideas if you can't come up with anything - it will get you to think about what you are actually selling.

Your headline message, on the front of your direct mail, must have impact and encourage the recipient to read on.

ASK A QUESTION?

"Do you want to know how to create ____?"

"Are you struggling to keep up-to-date with ____?"

"What are the top 10 reasons most ____ fail or succeed?"

"When did you last check ____?"

"Did you know that ____?"

"How many times do you find yourself ____?"

"Do you want to discover the secrets of ____?"

TELL THEM WHAT TO DO

"Discover how you can ____"

"Let us show you how you can ____"

"Unlock your potential with our ____"

"Get rid of ____ worries for good"

"10 Ways to… save/increase/gain/enhance/reduce/improve"

"Uncover the secret of ____"

"Discover three powerful ways of ____"

BE SENSATIONAL

"Revealed! A proven way to ____"

"Breakthrough system that can _____
Be among the first to discover its benefits"

"Unleash your potential with our amazing ____"

"Create amazing ___ with our ___"

"Turn your website into ___ with our ___"

"Unlock the secrets of the most successful ____"

"Explode your sale revenues with ____"

Whatever hook or headline message you use, ask yourself: "If I received this, would I read any further?" You have only a few seconds to get the attention of the person opening the direct mail.

You need a compelling hook, something intriguing that entices them to find out more.

Write down as many compelling headlines and hooks that you can think of for your direct mail:

Step 4 – The Medium

You have established why you are sending out a direct mail, who you are sending it to, and the main hook or headline to pique the recipients' interest. Now, what about the medium? Who said direct mail had to be a sales letter printed on your headed paper?

There are hundreds of ways to get people's attention and they aren't all paper-based. Let your imagination run wild and think about things that would grab your attention. If you received a box, packet or parcel, wouldn't you be more interested in opening it than a plain envelope?

Here are some real-life ideas to get you going:

THE VIEW-MASTER

This was sent to businesses to publicise the opening of a new airport. Rather than send out a simple brochure or letter, they tried to think of a way to get people to take a proper a look at what the airport had to offer.

Just think...

✓ You would open it

✓ The medium makes you want to look at the airport and pass it round to colleagues to take a look

✓ When you look through the viewfinder it has pictures and strong messages about the benefits of the airport

✓ An invitation to an open day is included with the direct mail and there is a reminder about it on one of the slides

THE PRINTING PRESS

A new printing press - isn't that exciting? This company treated it like the arrival of a new baby with a birth announcement:

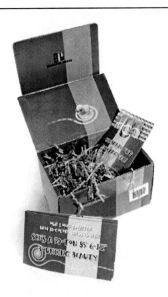

"It's a Girl – She is a 90 ton, 85ft 6in beauty!"

Just think...

✓ You would open it

✓ There is an invitation to go and see "the new baby" and to find out all about her

✓ There are confectionery cigars to celebrate the new arrival

---

MARKETING HIT

We used this one when we started in business. We bought miniature bottles of Tequila and Tabasco sauce, added a shot glass, packed them in a postal tube and included the following instructions:

    1. Take tequila and pour into glass
    2. Add dash of Tabasco
    3. Drink!

If you want a hit like this for your marketing, then call us NOW for your free Marketing Health Check

---

Here are some more ideas to get your creative juices flowing:

- Re-brand some tea, coffee or chocolate with your company name – Take a break and review your _____. Is it working for you?

- Send a mobile phone holder that looks like a deckchair. It will sit on the recipient's desk and the hook can be: Relax. Let us take care of your _____.

- Send a branded miniature tape measure – Does your _____ measure up?

- Branded calculator – include a simple sum and get them to calculate the cost of their _____ – Is your _____ providing the returns you want? Is it working for you?

- Torch – Are you in the dark about _____

- Transformer toys – We will transform your _____

- Magnifying glass – We focus on your business so you can _____

- Mints – Get the "extra strong" results you are looking for...

The possibilities are endless. If you are still finding it difficult, try using the ideas box approach in *Chapter 5*.

If you don't want to take the package approach, you can still achieve great things with paper. All you have to do is create something that is visually appealing and has that hook on the front. Here is an example that we used to great effect for a seminar:

Here is the front cover…

How can **marketing** give you the business you want…?

A FREE seminar that gives you the

to **unlocking** your marketing power!

Here is the back…

This management seminar from Leeds Chamber and Brighter Marketing will give you the knowledge and skills you need to help you address your marketing challenges and help to give you the business you want.

Why should you attend?

- **Increase your marketing knowledge,** discover what marketing can and can't do for your business
- **Save time,** and learn how to use marketing tools to your advantage
- **Gain marketing confidence,** learn the secrets of how to connect with prospects & customers
- **Reduce marketing stress,** find out why people buy and why psychology is important
- **Enhance your company image,** by developing your brand for success
- **Improve brand awareness,** rate your strategic IQ and understand how vision can drive marketing power

There is no quick fix to marketing your business, but by attending this seminar you will learn what really works and how to maximise your company's marketing potential.

Who should attend:

This invaluable, high-level seminar is aimed at those who are responsible for the future direction of your business, including;

- **CEOs/Managing Directors**
- **Finance Directors**
- **Sales and Marketing Directors**
- **Sales and Marketing Managers**

FREE Marketing Inspiration Cards

All those attending will receive complimentary Marketing Inspiration Cards that will help you assess and plan your marketing. They offer guidance and inspiration to help you expand your marketing knowledge and provide tips to help you connect effectively with your customers.

Leeds Chamber

IN BUSINESS FOR LEEDS

Leeds Chamber works with its partners to position Leeds as a key business location, by providing a wide range of products and services to support the growth and development of local businesses.

brightermarketing

Brighter Marketing are a proactive, experienced and motivational marketing company with the capability and focused expertise to help businesses unlock their marketing power.

Here is the response part...

Priority Registration

This important seminar will help you assess you current marketing situation and outline the way forward for marketing success. Places are limited, so make sure you reserve you place today.

Jon Smith
ABC Company
Happy House
6 Mirth Lane
Leeds
LS16 7YU

Simply complete this form and fax back to us on ₁
0113 247 1111

Alternatively speak to our events team on 0113 247 0000 to find out more and book your place.

Please amend if your details are incorrect

Tel: Fax:

Email:

Please reserve me ___ places on the following seminar:

27th January 2007

Village Hotel
186 Otley Road
Headlingley
LS16 5PR

9:00am -12pm

I wish to bring the following colleagues:

Name:

Position:

Name:

Position:

Leeds Chamber   brightermarketing

Obviously, we didn't design it ourselves - we got expert help from a direct mail agency that is used to working on direct mail and worked with us on this Seven-step System to provide the extra impetus we needed. If you are in any doubt about your ability to design a direct mail piece, we recommend you work with a creative agency. *Chapter 12* looks at choosing an agency.

Write down ideas for how to make your direct mail appealing – think beyond a simple sales letter.

Step 5 – The Content

You have hooked the recipient with a great headline, now deliver on it. Make the content of your direct mail compelling and interesting. Guide the reader towards what you want them to do.

Here are some tips to help you plan what you need to communicate after the hook but before Step 6, the Call to Action:

Be clean and clear – Don't clutter the mailer with too much text or try to communicate too much. Just give them the key benefits and avoid technical detail at all cost.

Follow-up – If your hook was...

*"Do you want to know how to create amazing
websites without HTML knowledge?"*

...tell them how they can do this. Give them a taster of what is possible with your product or service. Take them through what they can do. Then lead them to the offer:

"To find out more, get our FREE Websites Made Easy Guide...."

Include images – Include diagrams or photos to support your written communications. They must be good quality and be there for a reason.

Five key questions – Ensure your content communicates and answers the five key questions outlined in *Chapter* 3. They are:

1. Why should the prospect want to read what you have written?
2. Why should they believe what you have to say?
3. Why should they do anything about what you are offering?
4. Why should they act now?
5. What are the three key things you must communicate?

Step 6 – Call To Action. What's In It For Me (WIIFM)

For your direct mail to be effective, it must provoke action. It can look great, be sent to the right person and have the right message, but if you don't tell the recipient what to do, all your effort will have been wasted.

In Step 1, you wrote down what you wanted to achieve by sending the direct mail. This is when you use it - to get the recipient to take action and get in touch with you.

Here are some tips to improve the response rate to your direct mail and get people to take action:

Include an image of the front cover of the guide or health check you are offering, make it real for them. Even if you are only going to send them a PDF, a visual reference is key, as it makes the offer tangible and they feel they are going to receive something of value.

Tell them what to do. This may sound simple, but telling the recipient what to do can have an amazing effect. For example:

- Simply tick the box and return the reply-paid envelope TODAY for your FREE guide to...
- Places are limited. Call us NOW to secure your place

- Take advantage of this amazing offer TODAY, we only have 100 guides to give away

- Download your guide in seconds. Go to *www.brightermarekting.com* for instant access to 10 Ways to Improve Your Marketing

- Last time we ran this offer, the response was amazing, so make sure you call us today to book your audit.

Make it easy for them to respond. For example, don't include an envelope with your address on it and expect them to put a stamp on it! Get a reply-paid licence from the Post Office so there is no cost for them to send their response back to you. You should offer more than one way for them to get in touch with you as the example here shows.

Simply tick the box and return the reply-paid envelope TODAY for your FREE guide to _____

If you want to get the guide even faster, there are four other ways to get in touch with us:

Call us:	0113 11112222
Fax us:	0113 11113333
Register Online:	www.brightermarketing.com/guide
Email us:	guide@brightermarketing.com

A good tip and an example. If you ask recipients to fill out their own address details, it can be difficult to decipher hand-writing. Consider including a sticker or print their details on the reply-paid card so all they have to do is tick the box, and change their details if they are incorrect in any way. When they fax or mail back the request, you will have the correct information. You can even leave the telephone number and email blank - it is amazing how many people fill them in. See the example over the page.

Please amend if details are incorrect

Mr John Smith
Happy Company
Mirth House
Chuckle Lane
Smiland
SM34 7SP

☐ **Yes – Send me a copy of the marketing inspiration cards TODAY**

Tel No: _____

Email: _____

In the book *'YES! 50 Secrets from the Science of Persuasion'*, the author refers to the fact that creating urgency is important when trying to encourage people to respond to marketing. A shopping channel hired Colleen Sotz, a renowned copywriter, to develop new scripts for their programmes. The small changes she made had a dramatic effect on response rates to their infomercials.

She simply changed...

"Operators are waiting to take your call, please call now"

...to...

"If operators are busy, please call again"

Response rates went through the roof after this simple change. The impression the audience got was that the products must be popular, and that explained why the operators would be busy. Think about how you can create urgency with your direct mail campaigns - what can you say that will prompt your target audience to take action?

Fulfilment. Consider getting help with fulfilment - better known as envelope stuffing - if you have larger amounts of direct mail. There are plenty of companies that will take care of inserting the direct mail into envelopes and posting them for you. So just bear in mind that you don't have to spend days putting together the direct mail and sticking on stamps or running envelopes through the franking machine.

Step 7 – The Follow-Up

This is the step many people forget about. They send out the direct mail, they get some response, send off the information or see who has downloaded the guide from the web page and then... nothing. In many cases nothing much happens once the initial responses have been received.

You must follow up your direct mail. There are two ways to do it.

First Follow-up: Call the people who responded to the direct mail after you have sent the information they requested. This is not a sales call – do not try to sell them anything at this stage. Just call them to confirm they received the information you sent and to find out if they found it useful. Chat to them, find out why they requested the guide. Were they having any particular problems? Do they have any particular challenges at the moment that prompted them to send for the guide? Just listen to them and then, if appropriate, you can suggest ways in which you could help them overcome their challenges.

"So John, as far as I understand it, your main challenges are X and Y, and you want to find a way that gives you the outcome you want which is Z. Is that right? OK – If I could help you do this, would you be interested? The guide we provided gives you top-level help, however, it sounds like you need more detailed assistance..."

If you don't follow up, you are depending on people to get in touch with you. They may have loved the guide, but just got busy and thought they would call you when they got a chance to talk about their particular challenge – but that chance never came. So make that call and maximise the effect of your direct mail.

Second Follow-up: Having sent out the direct mail in small batches, as we recommended, and, having talked to all the respondents, the second follow-up is to those who didn't respond.

Call them to confirm they received the direct mail and to ask if they would they like to receive the guide. Let them know what a great response you had and tell them you don't want them to miss out. Although these calls are not as warm as the ones to the people who did respond, if you sent out a memorable piece of direct mail, there is every chance they will remember it. Perhaps they were busy and forgot to respond. If you call to remind them, it will prompt action.

Remember to do Step 7 – it can make a big difference.

EMAIL MARKETING – FINDING NEW PROSPECTS

Email marketing can be a cost-effective, quick and easy way to market your products and services to prospective clients. However, it comes with a big health warning:

> ### Sending emails to people who haven't requested them is SPAM. Doing this will seriously damage your company's reputation and image.

So, how can you use email marketing safely and effectively?

There are only three ways and they are:

1. **Build Your Own List of Prospects**
   You can collect email addresses from your website by asking visitors if they want to subscribe to receive information from you. In addition, you can ask prospects you meet if you can add them to your mailing list. This can be time-consuming but it is worthwhile. However, remember wherever you get prospects' email addresses, you must secure permission from each of them to email information from your company.

2. **Work With a Reputable Email Marketing Company**
   Specialist email companies have lists of recipients who have opted to receive email information about certain types of products or services, IT security or employment law, for example. They will not give you access to their lists and will normally invite you to run an advert or banner on one of their mailings which is being sent to your target market.

3. **Joint Partner**
   Find companies that have complementary products or
   services to the ones you provide and have a list of subscribers
   who have agreed to receive information from third parties.
   These can be difficult to find and you should choose any
   partner carefully - make sure their list is bona fide and
   confirm that you have permission to email their subscribers.

7 Step Email Marketing System

The rules that apply to direct marketing also apply to email
marketing. If you plan to email individuals, use the same seven-step
system to ensure you get the response you want. You may want to
modify it for email:

Step 1 – What Do You Want To Achieve?

Again, think about what you want the recipient to do - link to a
landing page on your website, call you, email you?

Step 2 – Your Target Audience

Ensure that you are sending the email message to the decision-maker
in your target market.

Step 3 – The Hook

You want them to open the email, so make the subject heading
compelling. Avoid the use of words such as "free" and
"complimentary" as these can be blocked by spam filters.

Step 4 – The Medium

This doesn't really apply here, but make sure that the email is short,
not cluttered and is on a white background

Step 5 – The Content

You have even less time to grab the reader's attention after they have
opened the email than you do with traditional direct mail - make
every word count and get your message across quickly.

Step 6 – The Call To Action Or WIIFM (What's In It For Me?)

Make the call to action easy to spot and simple for the recipient to act
on. If you have a link to your website you must create a specific page
– a landing page – for visitors to arrive at when they click the link.

This is crucial, especially if they want to download a guide or software. The page should refer to the offer and thank them for responding, so they know they are in the right place. Then you can tell them how to access the guide or software. For more information on landing pages, see *Chapter 8*.

Step 7 – Follow-Up

You must follow-up - it can make a huge difference to the success of your campaign. However, this may not be possible if you are using an email company or a partner's list.

Email Software

If you are considering sending out emails yourself, there are plenty of cost-effective ways to do it that will make your company look professional and enable personalisation of individual emails from you.

Never send an email with all the recipients' email addresses in the To or CC box. If you do decide to use Outlook or another mail package, then you should at the very least hide the addresses in the BCC box. More importantly you must give recipients the option to unsubscribe from your emails at any time.

The online email companies listed below provide an easy way to send professional-looking emails. They are all reputable, will manage your list and remove anyone who clicks through to unsubscribe. More importantly, all have tracking features so you know who has opened your emails and clicked through to your landing page - invaluable information for follow-up!

- *www.livewirecampaign.com*
- *www.dotmailer.co.uk*
- *www.newzapp.co.uk*
- *www.aweber.com*
- *www.icontact.com*
- *www.infusionsoft.com*
- *www.constantcontact.com*

PR – GETTING KNOWN AS AN EXPERT

PR can work wonders for your company, but getting results takes a lot more than just sending out some press releases. PR is all about getting coverage in the publications read by your target market. It won't give you instant sales leads, but it can generate interest over time and help set you up as an expert.

Positive coverage in key publications read by the decision-makers in your target market can be very effective in raising your profile. However, for PR to be really effective, there should be a sustained approach that wins coverage on a regular basis and gets your company known in the press and trade publications that are relevant to you.

It's All About Contacts

To achieve successful PR coverage, you or your marketing team must have, or be committed to creating and maintaining, relationships with the editors, journalists and freelancers who write the copy and place the stories. They decide what goes into a publication, what articles to write or commission and who to quote. If they don't know about you and your company's expertise, sending them the odd press release won't produce the coverage you seek.

If you are not committed to doing this or simply don't have the time or resources, find a PR consultant or agency to do it on your behalf. They will already have the contacts you need or will know how to get them.

What is PR?

As we said, issuing press releases is only a small part of the PR process. If you want regular press coverage for your company, consider the following actions.

Identify a short list of relevant titles you want to target, titles your target market will be reading. This should include local press, trade press, online publications and national newspapers. Make sure you know the contacts at each of the publications – e.g. editor, news editor, features editor, travel writer, technology reporter - by name. This will help you to forge relationships and ensure that your or your PR agency's time is focused on the appropriate publications.

Track forward features. Most publications will provide a list of the features they are planning over the following six months and the name of the journalist to contact with relevant content or information. Once you have identified opportunities from the forward features list, contact the journalist with offers of content or comment.

Make your press releases count. When you issue a press release, make it newsworthy and interesting to the readership of your target publication. Only send a press release when you have something worthwhile to say. Try to write an attention-grabbing headline. Do not call the journalist to see if they have received it - they are usually working to a deadline and your call will be an inconvenience. If they want to use it, they will let you know.

Find out how each journalist or publication prefers to receive press releases. Some want hard copy, others prefer email with the text pasted into the body of the email, others prefer Word attachments. It is worth checking what picture formats are preferred, too. Always send the appropriate format to each journalist or writer.

Under "notes for editors", provide contact details of a spokesperson and some basic information about your company and attach any images associated with the press release.

To find out more about how to write a press release, go to *www.prwebdirect.com/pressreleasetips.php*

Make yourself the expert. Always have a regular spokesperson available to comment or provide information for journalists on a particular subject. Expert comment can add weight to an article, so always be ready to comment and be confident in the answers you give. Always deliver on time and be reliable. Send them a personal thank you if they publish your comments.

Pitch a story. Magazines and publications want to fill their pages with articles their readers will be interested in. If you have a good story idea, get in touch and let the journalists know about it. Ideas include an interesting case study, a "how to" guide, interview with an expert, the results of a survey you have commissioned.

PR is not an exact science, but if you put in some effort and/or work with a good PR professional or agency, it can reap rewards.

ADVERTISING – SEVEN TOP TIPS AND INSIDER SECRETS

Advertising can be expensive, so always think about what you are trying to communicate before you part with your cash. If you are selling PCs and advertise regularly in PC Advisor, which has a readership of 52,504 people who are interested in buying PCs, this may be an effective way of marketing your products. Basically, if your product lends itself to "selling off the page", do it. If it doesn't, think again!

Advertising often gives what appear to be disappointing results in the B2B world. When was the last time you saw an advert and responded directly to it? It does happen, but it usually takes more than one advert in one publication and, like direct mail, there has to be a strong call to action.

For advertising to be effective, it has to appear regularly, building up reader-recognition over time. Never be tempted by a smooth-talking advertising sales rep to place a one-off advert in a publication - the chances are it won't do anything for you.

However, if advertising is for you, here are our top seven tips.

1 – Proof of Circulation & Readership

Make sure the publications in which you have chosen to advertise are read by your target market. Ask for their ABC (Audit Bureau of Circulation) figures, which give their official audited circulation and a description of who their readers are. For more information, or if the publisher can't give you access to their figures, go to *www.abc.org.uk* (UK) or *www.accessabc.com* (US).

2 – Negotiate on Price

Never take the first price offered. Publications need advertisers and they regularly have spare advert slots, whether they admit it or not. You can tell this by seeing how many adverts they run for their own associated products or services. They don't need to run these adverts and normally only do this when they can't fill the space with paid-for advertising. Before you agree to any price for advertising, get the publication's rate card - they should supply one on request, or you can find it on their website or in their media pack. If you don't know the starting point for negotiations, how can you know if you are getting a good deal?

On the rate card, they will offer a series discount for booking six or 12 months of adverts, but this is just the published discount rate. Advertising executives can offer more, and will – all you have to do is ask. They want guaranteed, booked advertising space, and if you can commit to 12 months you are in a much better position to negotiate. Don't be afraid to ask for a much higher discount. You may not get what you ask for and have to compromise, but you should always get more than the standard series discount.

We should know - we bought advertising for years and never paid the rate card price. If you get to know your advertising executive and build a good relationship with them, they might throw in a free advert here and there when they have some space and give you first refusal on supplement or feature sponsorships.

3 – Negotiate on Position
Try to secure a regular place in the publication for your adverts. Aim for a right-hand page, early in the publication.

Why? We naturally look to the right-hand page when turning over pages. We also tend to read the news pages first and they are at the start of most publications. If you are in the same or a similar position for the next 12 months, regular readers will get used to seeing your advert, recognition increases and, if your call to action is strong enough, a percentage of readers should respond sooner or later.

The only time this doesn't apply is if there is a feature or section related to your industry. Your advert should be positioned in or near this to ensure that while the reader's mind is on a particular subject your advert appears before them.

4 – Choose The Size of Advert That Suits You, Not The Advertiser

What size advert should you go for? A single page, double-page spread, half-page, or a slim-line running along the bottom of the page?

It mostly depends on what you can afford and what works for you. We steer clear of double-page spreads - they are expensive and readers don't really look at them, they just turn the page. Full-page adverts are okay but for the best effect they should be on the right hand side, opposite a news page. Half page adverts have their place but, again, they should be below an article, not above another half-page advert.

5 – Don't Be Seduced by a "Late Deal"

An advertising executive calls you with a late deal. One of their advertisers has pulled out and they can offer you the space at half-price if you can commit to taking it before the end of the day as the print deadline is approaching. Before you jump into this amazing deal, use the following checklist:

- Is the publication read by the decision-makers you want to target?
- Check the rate card price - is it really half-price?
- Do you have an advert you can use? If not, will there be another cost in creating one or re-sizing artwork?
- What will be achieved by placing this one-off advert? If you weren't planning to do it, will it really have an impact on your sales leads?

If you can answer 'yes' to these questions and you really want to place the advert, you should still negotiate on price. If they do have a deadline approaching, they will take the best price they can get, rather than leave the space empty or fill it with one of their own adverts.

6 – Strong Hook & Call To Action

As with direct mail and email marketing, you must have a strong headline or hook and call to action if your advert is to stand out in the publication. Less is always more in advertising. This is what to do:

- Make your hook or headline stand out.
- Make it clear and easy to read.

- Include a relevant or eye-catching image.
- Identify two or three key benefits.
- Have a strong call to action, e.g., offer a guide, "white paper" or audit.
- Make sure your telephone number or website landing page for the offer is clearly displayed.

7 – Get professional input

If you want a really effective advert, one that stands out, get the help of a professional designer. You don't need to go to an expensive ad agency - there will be plenty of freelance designers in your area who will do a great job for you. Lots of freelance designers have worked for the large ad agencies at one time or another. To help find one, go to *www.elance.com* for details of all sorts of freelancers who specialise in a range of design skills. Or just find a local agency that specialises in advertising, look at their previous work and, if you like what you see, work with them.

Over the page is an example of a very simple but effective advert that worked for us in the past, it didn't generate loads of leads but did support our other marketing activities and did bring in some enquiries.

A word of caution: if you are going to work with an agency or professional designer be very clear and precise about what you want to achieve. If they don't give you an advertising brief to complete or to work through with them, do one of your own before you start working with them. We have provided a simple template on the following two pages to help you. Also, read *Chapter 12* which tells you how to choose an agency.

Advertising Brief

| **OBJECTIVE** |
| What are you advertising – the company and/or product/service?
What do you want the advertising to achieve? |
| **PRODUCT OR SERVICE** |
| What are the key product/service benefits? |
| **TARGET AUDIENCE** |
| Whom is the advertising targeted?
What does the target audience already know about your products and services? |
| **CURRENT PERCEPTIONS** |
| How is your company product or service perceived in the marketplace? |
| **DESIRED PERCEPTIONS** |
| How do you want the company/product/service to be perceived? |
| **INSIGHT** |
| Why should the audience want to respond to the advertising? |
| **WHAT MAKES THIS UNIQUE?** |
| How is this proposition different from what the competition offers? |
| **DESIRED ACTION** |
| What single-minded response do you want from the audience?
What do you want the audience to do as a result of the advertising? |
| **TONE** |
| Is there a tone of voice or personality/image you need to maintain, enhance, replace or create? |
| **GUIDELINES/MANDATORY INCLUSIONS** |
| Are there any mandatory (e.g., legal, practical or product-related) inclusions?
What logos/brands must be included? |
| **TIMESCALES** |
| What are the timescales and any artwork deadlines? |
| **MEDIA AND TECHNICAL/DESIGN SPECIFICATION** |
| Where will the adverts be appearing?
What size is required? Have technical/mechanical details been supplied? |

SUCCESSFUL SEMINARS – THE SIX-STEP SYSTEM

Running your own seminar or breakfast briefing can be a very effective way to meet the decision-makers in your target market face-to-face and give you an opportunity to demonstrate your expertise.

For a seminar to be successful, it must be educational and not a thinly disguised sales pitch for your products or services. Whatever you decide to talk about, it must be useful, educational and informative and, most importantly, the attendees must feel they have learned something new and useful.

Here is our six-step system to running a successful seminar.

Step 1 – Content, Title And Presenters

First, decide on the content of your seminar. If you can't decide what to talk about, the following may help:

- Look to your clients for inspiration. What challenges have you helped them overcome? Are there key issues that come up time and time again?
- Have there been changes in legislation that are important to your industry that you could talk about?
- Has there been a change in the industry sector that you could talk about, e.g. the take-up of a new technology?
- Are there specific subjects on which you are an expert - accounting for small businesses, legalities of building contracts, direct mail, creativity, finding finance for businesses?

Once you know what you are going to talk about, there are lots of ways to present your information. Here are a few ideas.

Presentation: If you take a "we talk, you listen" approach, make sure the topics will hold your audience's attention. Where possible, incorporate some interactivity, ask questions and take polls from the floor. In this way you will involve the audience, giving your presentation more credibility.

If you use PowerPoint, it should support the presentation – don't just read bullet points off the screen. *Chapter 7* offers more hints and tips on creating great PowerPoint presentations that deliver.

Forum or workshop: People are invited to take part in a forum to discuss a particular topic. You lead the forum and enable the participants to talk and provide examples of the challenges they face, sparking discussion on how you and the other participants can help them overcome their challenges.

Examples or case studies: Present examples within a subject area and bring them to life with case studies or demonstrations of how particular challenges were overcome. For example, a firm of solicitors who specialised in employment law developed a mock tribunal that highlighted key areas where employers can go wrong and included questions afterwards.

Chalk and talk: This is a more interactive style of presenting particularly suited to the IT industry. It is a good way to demonstrate your expert knowledge on a particular subject. Invite the participants to supply questions before the event, then provide answers to the challenges using no more than a white board and pen. The audience benefits from learning about real-life issues and problems and can also see that you are an expert. As you work through the challenges, invite comments from the floor and ask questions to ensure that everyone benefits from the exercise and it isn't just you talking and drawing.

Joint venture: Developing a seminar with a partner who provides complementary products and services to yours can be a great way of covering a subject area. For example, an IT security company could have a joint venture with a team of lawyers who are specialists in cyber crime or a recruitment agency could develop a seminar with a firm of HR consultants.

Joint venture seminars give more credibility to presentations – the audience is provided with valuable information from a team of experts, not just one company.

A word of caution: always develop the seminar content together with your joint venture partner and be united on what you want to communicate to the audience. This is vitally important as you don't want to provide conflicting information to the target audience.

Networking time = food: You will want to meet the decision-makers you have invited to the event, and the best way to do this can be over some food. If yours is a morning event, provide breakfast prior to the presentation; if it lasts all morning, provide lunch afterwards. This will give you and your team time to network and find out more about their businesses. It also gives the delegates a chance to network with each other.

Title: Give your event a catchy title, something that will stimulate interest and encourage the decision-makers you are targeting to attend your seminar. Here are some titles of successful seminars we and our clients have run:

- Make Your Business Amazing – Avoiding the Seven Deadly Sins
- How Marketing Can Give You The Business You Want
- Why Your Employees Are the Biggest Threat to your IT Security
- Persuasion and Charisma – The Secrets of Good Management
- Strategy v Tactics – What Every Manager Needs to Know

When choosing a title, ask yourself if you would want to attend a seminar by that name? Does the title compel you to attend? If your answer is "Err, no", think again.

Presenter: You can have the best content in the world and the most amazing title, but if the seminar is given by someone who is not a great presenter, it can all fall apart very quickly. We have attended seminars that promised great things, but people started to fall asleep after half-an-hour!

If you are giving a presentation, your presentation skills must be good. They don't have to be dazzling, but you must be able to hold your audience's attention and answer questions confidently. If you know this isn't the case, you have two options:

1. Get some presentation skills training and then practice, practice, practice.

2. Find someone who has a track record of presenting and is knowledgeable enough to answer questions from the floor to give the presentation.

Step 2 – Location, Location, Location

Not everyone thinks enough about the venue when they are planning a seminar - your choice of location can affect how you are perceived. Your seminar must be accessible and the venue must meet your needs. Always visit the venue to make sure it is right for your seminar - the brochure pictures may look great, but they are no substitute for a site visit. Here is a checklist to use when selecting a venue:

☐ Does it have sufficient free parking? Is it near a railway station or underground stop? Can delegates get there without having to find parking or walk a long distance?

☐ Is the venue well known? Sometimes an interesting venue, such as a racetrack, stately home or famous hotel, can stimulate curiosity and increase the number of people who attend.

☐ Does it have good presentation facilities? Consider the following:
   o Different sizes of rooms, in case the number of people wanting to attend increases or decreases
   o Projector and screen
   o Laptop
   o Ability to plug in your own laptop
   o Hand-held PowerPoint advancer
   o Wi-fi – or high-speed internet connection
   o Sound system, adequate speakers and microphone, including tie/lapel microphones
   o Lectern
   o White board
   o Flip chart
   o Flexible seating, so delegates can sit theatre-style or classroom-style depending on your requirements
   o Good ventilation or air conditioning

- o   Natural daylight, total blackout or lighting control
- o   Video/DVD facilities
- o   Refreshment and catering - what's included in the price?
- o   Overhead projector
- o   35mm slide projector
- o   CD player
- o   Break-out rooms

☐   Are there good facilities for disabled people?

☐   Is the venue experienced at staging presentations and conferences? Is there a person or team to liaise with?

☐   If the venue is providing food, ask to sample some of it to ensure it is suitable. Can they provide options to meet different dietary needs?

☐   Where is the presentation room in relation to the entrance? Will there be adequate signage to your room and acknowledgement of the delegates as they enter the building?

☐   Can you set up a welcome and registration desk in a prominent position?

Step 3 – The Invitation – WIIFM (What's In It For Me?)

You have your subject, a title, a presenter and the venue. All you need now are delegates. Whether you send a direct mail invitation or an email notification of your event, the seven-step direct mail system outlined in *Chapter 7* still applies. And you should consider the following when writing the copy for your invitation:

Why Attend?

What are the compelling reasons for people to take time out of their busy days to attend your seminar? What's in it for them?

Who Should Attend?

Make clear whom the seminar is for. Although you will be sending the invitation only to your target market, you should reassure them that they are the right person to attend.

What Will They Learn?

Tell them what they will learn as a result of attending.

What Is The Call To Action?
What should they do right now to ensure they get a place on this seminar?

How Do They Respond?
Make it easy for them to respond - can they call, email, fill out a web form or send back a reply-paid card?

When Should You Send Out The Invitation?
Send the invitations four to six weeks before the event. This gives delegates time to make space in their diaries and leaves you plenty of time to finish planning the seminar. If the invitation is enticing enough, you can expect an acceptance rate of between 2 and 7%. Taking a mid-point response rate of around 4%, you can work out how many individuals are likely to want to attend and book the room before you send out the invitation. Get an assurance from your venue that, should the numbers go up or down, you can still be accommodated in a suitable room. You shouldn't turn anyone away from a seminar because it is "fully booked" – always find a way to enable everyone who wants to attend to be there. Having gone to all the effort of getting people to attend, the last thing you want is for them to be turned away.

To Charge or Not To Charge?
Someone who has paid to attend is more likely to turn up on the day than someone who hasn't paid - they have made financial commitment to attend. However, a charge could dissuade some people from attending. If you do charge, it is probably best to keep it to a nominal fee of £25 or so, which you should explain is to cover costs. Also charging for your seminar will require more effort on your part as you will have to arrange to take credit card payments.

Step 4 – Pre-Seminar
When delegates start responding and requesting places at your seminar, use this checklist to ensure you do everything you can to make your event a success. This is a good starting point, but you may want to add more, depending on the type of event you are running.

- ☐ Record delegates' details on a spreadsheet or in a database as soon as they accept your invitation.
- ☐ Post or email details of the event to delegates - registration time, an agenda and details of how to find the venue. Include a map and satellite navigation details or rail and flight information if applicable.
- ☐ If you are providing food, establish whether they have any dietary requirements.
- ☐ Prepare a checklist of what to take with you on the day.
- ☐ Print badges for each of the delegates.
- ☐ Prepare information packs, guides, pads, pens and/or giveaways to use on the day.
- ☐ Rehearse presentations. Watch the presentations of any joint venture partners to ensure they are suitable. If this isn't possible, check the PowerPoint versions of their presentations.
- ☐ Check PowerPoint presentations for errors or problems with animations.
- ☐ Check and prepare any technical equipment or software.
- ☐ Call everyone on the delegate list the day before the seminar to confirm their attendance - this should give you an idea of how many people are likely to turn up, especially if the seminar is free.
- ☐ Brief relevant company employees about the seminar and their roles during breaks and during breakfast or lunch. Tell them if there are any individuals you particularly want them to talk to.
- ☐ Call the venue to check that all the facilities you requested are in place and to confirm the numbers for catering.
- ☐ Create a registration list to check off the delegates as they arrive and so that you know who has turned up
- ☐ Write thank you letters or emails for those who attended the seminar to be sent out afterwards. Write a different version for those who didn't attend.
- ☐ Prepare delegate feedback sheets to help you gauge the success and content of your presentations. A sample is provided here…

Seminar Feedback Form

At _____ we want to ensure that all our seminars and events provide you with the information you need and are of consistent quality. Your comments are important to us and we would appreciate it if you could complete this seminar feedback form which helps us to ensure we are meeting our delegates' requirements.

Name: _____

Company: _____

ABOUT THE VENUE

Please could you rate the following by placing an X in the appropriate box.
1=Poor 2=Unsatisfactory 3=Satisfactory 4=Good 5=Excellent

VENUE	1	2	3	4	5
1. Directions to the venue					
2. Initial greeting during registration					
3. Quality of refreshments and food					
4. Comfort and facilities available at venue					
Additional comments regarding the venue:					

ABOUT THE PRESENTATIONS

Please could you rate the following by placing an X in the appropriate box.
1=Poor 2=Unsatisfactory 3=Satisfactory 4=Good 5=Excellent

PRESENTATION #1	1	2	3	4	5
Content					
Presenter					
PRESENTATION #2	1	2	3	4	5
Content					
Presenter					
PRESENTATION #3	1	2	3	4	5
Content					
Presenter					
Additional comments regarding the presentations:					

ABOUT THE BREAKOUT SESSIONS

Only complete this section if you attended the breakout sessions.
Please could you rate the following by placing an X in the appropriate box?
1=Poor 2=Unsatisfactory 3=Satisfactory 4=Good 5=Excellent

BREAKOUT #1	1	2	3	4	5
Information you gained					
Knowledge of facilitator					
BREAKOUT #2	1	2	3	4	5
Information you gained					
Knowledge of facilitator					
BREAKOUT #3	1	2	3	4	5
Information you gained					
Knowledge of facilitator					
Additional comments regarding the breakout sessions:					

Thank you for completing this seminar feedback form. If you would like further information on any of our products and services, please tick the relevant boxes below.

- ☐ Product 1
- ☐ Product 2
- ☐ Product 3
- ☐ Service 1

If you did not hand in this feedback form to a representative at the event, please fax it back to us on _____ or scan and email to _____

Step 5 – On The Day

Always arrive before your delegates. If you are running a breakfast seminar, be there as soon as the venue opens. If it is a hotel, or there is one nearby, consider staying the night before so that you and the team are ready to do business.

What you need to do on the big day - here is a checklist to make sure everything goes to plan:

- ☐ Meet your contact at the venue to confirm everything you need is in place. If it isn't, get it sorted ASAP.

- ☐ Test all the equipment - make sure projectors are working, the sound system is set at the right volume and the seating arrangements are as you want them. Familiarise yourself and any presenters with your surroundings. If you have time, practice your presentation.
- ☐ Set up your registration desk – have it ready at least half-an-hour before registration time. Lay out name badges in alphabetical order according to last names.
- ☐ Have someone at the entrance to the venue to greet delegates and direct them to your room.
- ☐ When delegates arrive at the registration desk, make sure they are greeted with a warm smile and words of welcome to the seminar. Give them their badge. Tell them where the tea/coffee or breakfast is.
- ☐ Have employees and presenters ready to greet delegates in the tea/coffee area. Get them to mingle and talk to people.
- ☐ Guide the delegates to their seats five minutes before the presentation is due to start. If there are no-shows, you should still start on time. Have someone wait outside to let any late arrivals into the seminar room as they arrive.
- ☐ Don't worry if some delegates don't turn up - often with free seminars the drop-out rate can be as high as 40%. This should be much lower if people have paid to attend
- ☐ When you open the seminar, thank the delegates for attending and give a brief introduction covering what they are about to learn. Tell them when you would like to take questions and how the seminar will be run. Tell them where the exits and toilets are.
- ☐ When you introduce each of the presenters, tell the audience a little bit about them and their expertise. This confirms to the audience that the speaker is an expert, someone who knows his/her subject.
- ☐ At the end, thank delegates for attending and ask them to complete feedback forms with an assurance that their views will be taken into consideration. Collect the forms from delegates as they leave the room.
- ☐ At the end or during breaks, guide the delegates to where you want them to go. These are opportunities for you and your employees to network with them.

Step 6 – Follow-up

This is a very important part of the seminar process: you must follow up every person who attended the seminar as well as those who didn't.

- ☐ The day after the seminar, send the letters or emails you pre-prepared in Step 3 to those who attended and to those who didn't. Thank them for attending and let them know you are available to help with their challenges. You could include an offer in the letter to those who attended, e.g. "As a thank you for attending the event, we would like to offer you an audit of your _____ with no obligation".

- ☐ Don't write to, but call people who you or your team made personal connections with at the event to continue the discussions you had about their particular issues or problems. This enables you to capitalise on hot leads quickly, rather than wait for them to receive a letter.

- ☐ Three or four days after sending the thank you letter, call the delegates who attended to find out what they thought of the seminar. Ask if you can be of further assistance or if they would like to take advantage of any promotion you offered.

- ☐ When you have exhausted the list of people who attended, call those who didn't. Give them some feedback about the event and find out if they would like to be kept informed about future events.

- ☐ Look at the feedback forms - they will provide an honest appraisal of the event and indications of what you might need to do to improve for next time.

If you have invested time, money and effort into staging a seminar, it is criminal not to follow-up - you can get so much more from the event by doing so. The delegates may have found the seminar really useful, but once they got back to their offices, they were busy and, although they meant to get in touch, often they just didn't find the time. Getting in touch by letter and phone is the best way to maximise your return from such an event.

EXHIBITIONS – FOUR-STEP APPROACH TO SUCCESS

Exhibitions can be excellent places to find new clients, meet existing clients and network with other companies in your industry. They offer speaking opportunities, a chance to meet journalists and opportunities to find out about the latest innovations in your marketplace.

However, they can be expensive and you must plan your exhibition strategy with military precision to ensure you achieve maximum return on investment. We meet many companies that have spent money on an exhibition, but didn't get anything out of it. Often, this is because they just turned up without really thinking about or planning how they would turn their stand into a magnet for clients.

There are four main steps to follow if you want your attendance at an exhibition to be a success. Take our word for it, they work. We attended numerous exhibitions across the UK, Europe and the USA for a number of years on behalf of the companies we worked for. Our experience enabled us to develop a system that worked, one that ensured we got a good return on investment.

Step 1 – What & Why
Step 1 can save you a lot of time, money and effort. It involves answering two questions honestly and will either prepare you for the next step or help you realise you don't actually need to attend this or any other exhibition.

Why do you want to attend The Widget Exhibition?
Think very carefully about why you want to go. Is it because everyone else is going? Is it because you always go? Perhaps you think you should go because there might be some decision-makers there who you want to meet? Is it the right exhibition for you? Will it really deliver the decision-makers you are looking for?

You need to know why you are attending the exhibition - going because everyone else is isn't a good enough reason.

Write Down The Reasons You Want To Attend The Exhibition:

If you decide you do want to attend the exhibition and you know why, think about what you want to achieve by attending. Do you want to raise awareness of your company, your products or services? Do you want to create leads for your products or services at the exhibition? Or do you want to a launch a new product?

Be precise about your goals, as they will drive the way you approach the exhibition and the marketing activities you undertake before, during and after the event. Remember, the cost of an exhibition includes much more than the stand space alone. You have to factor in:

- Stand design and furniture
- Cost of employees attending the show – travel, accommodation
- Promotional and marketing costs
- Other costs such as electricity, lights, etc, to the stand

You should be very aware of the costs versus what you want to achieve by attending and be confident that you are likely to get a good return on investment. Think about whether you could get the same amount of coverage by sending out a direct mail or running your own seminar, both of which could cost much less.

Write Down What You Want To Achieve:
What are your goals and your expected return on investment? What will the exhibition deliver?

When you know why you want to attend the exhibition and have identified your goals, make a few final checks before you commit:

- What is the exhibition's track record? Ask for an analysis of last year's attendees. This will show you how many people attended, what type of companies they were from, and, more importantly, if your target decision-makers were there.

- Call a cross-section of the exhibitors who attended last year and find out what they thought of it.

- Look at the website promoting the exhibition. Is it professional? Does it encourage people to register?

- Ask the organisers how they will be marketing the event? Will it go off with a bang or like a damp squib?

- Where is the exhibition? If it is in London, many of the attendees will be from England. Is this really useful to you when most of your client base is in Scotland? Can you provide a product or service to the people who are likely to be attracted to a London exhibition?

- What else are the organisers offering in terms of publicity, sponsorship, speaking opportunities, advertising in the pre-show catalogue, etc?

- How much does it cost and what is included? Remember, the floor space or the basic shell scheme is just the beginning. No matter how small or large your stand, it needs to look attractive and this will incur further cost.

If you are happy the exhibition is for you, consider this one last point:

You don't have to take a stand at an exhibition to benefit from it. If your objective it to raise awareness and network with other exhibitors, you can achieve this just by going to the exhibition and meeting people, securing a speaking slot and arranging to meet journalists there on the day. You get the benefits of attending, without the cost. There is no law that says you have to take a stand.

Step 2 – Pre-Exhibition

When you have decided to take a stand, get planning. Here are the key points that will help you make the most of the time you are there, whether it's one, two, three or even four days.

Booking Space

The sooner you book your space, the better. If the exhibition is an annual event, past exhibitors will usually have secured first refusal on the best spaces as soon as the previous year's exhibition closed. This doesn't mean the only spaces available are in poor positions - not everyone re-books, some companies increase their stand space, some reduce it, so there will still be plenty of good spaces available. However, if you leave it till the last minute to book, you won't get the best spot or be included in promotional material sent out before and during the show by the organisers.

Size and Location

What size of stand do you need? Where should it be located? The answers largely depend on the type of exhibition you are attending.

Some smaller exhibitions have only one type of stand space: a pre-built scheme with walls and panels in various sizes from 4m2 up to

12m2, so your choice is limited. However, some larger exhibitions offer everything from 4m2 up to 100m2 and beyond, with a choice of space only or pre-built schemes.

The size of stand you choose will probably depend on your budget. If you book space only, you will have to budget for having a stand designed and installed. Bigger doesn't always mean better - you can do a lot with a small stand space, as long as it is in a good location.

There are no golden rules for finding the perfect stand location; every exhibition layout is different. However, with a little research, you can select stand space in a good location that will be seen by most of the attendees.

- Ask for an exhibition map that shows which stands have been reserved and the ones that are still available. Check where the majority of the stands have been reserved. If there is a cluster of them, it is likely these are high-traffic areas or that larger organisations have taken stands there. See if any stands of the size you want are available in this area. If not, ask the organisers if they will split stands or merge two spaces together to give you the size you want.

- Identify the entrances and exits, coffee bars and rest areas. People get hungry and thirsty and will find their way to at least one of these areas as they walk round the exhibition - and everyone has to enter and leave the exhibition at some point.

- Consider attending another exhibition with a similar layout to the one you plan to exhibit at to find out how people move around and where the hot spots are.

- Ask the exhibition organisers to suggest a good space for you. They are keen to sell you space, and it is in their interests to provide a location that will encourage you to re-book the following year.

- Ask exhibitors who attended the previous year where the best positions were and how traffic flowed around the stands.

Exhibition Manual

When you have booked your space, you will be sent an exhibition manual that explains everything you need to know about the exhibition, from where press rooms will be, to how to order electricity and lights for your stand. Before you do anything else, read it! It will contain important information that could save you a great deal of time and effort. It will include:

- Build-up and break-down times for the stands
- Show opening and closing times
- Car parking facilities and vehicle passes
- Details of accommodation and preferential hotel rates for overnight accommodation
- Deadlines for company profile submissions for the show catalogues
- Rules and regulations on what you can and can't do to your stand or what the height or other limitations are on your stand design
- Shell-scheme stand specification - what you get, e.g., walls, carpet
- How to order electricity, lights and water for your stand from the main contractors
- Freight forwarding companies – you will need one if you are shipping your stand from abroad
- Information and order forms for passes for employees
- Details of stand cleaning services
- Deadlines for advertising and sponsorship opportunities
- Speaking opportunities and who to contact
- How to order food and the catering companies available
- How to order furniture or plants for your stand
- How to order data capture software to record visitors
- Where the organisers can be found at the show
- Where to meet journalists and the location of the press room
- Information on sound levels allowed on your stand
- How to order audio-visual equipment
- How to order flowers and plants for your stand

- How to order internet connectivity or broadband
- How to order a phone for your stand
- How to order floor coverings if you have space only
- Information about insurance you may need to take out
- How to order complimentary tickets to send to clients and prospects
- Where to find the exhibition shop - in case you forget an essential, like Velcro
- Emergency and security procedures

Pay attention to the deadlines for everything you need, and get your orders or information back to the organisers in good time. Remember, ordering after the deadline or while you are at the exhibition will result in higher costs and you may have to wait for a contractor or not get the item or service at all.

Stand Design: Keep It Simple
The design of your stand is important: it can have a huge impact on how you are perceived by attendees and how it communicates your marketing messages.

Before getting on to designs or themes for your stand, think about what you want to achieve and the marketing messages you want to communicate at the exhibition. Keep it simple. When attendees walk past your stand, you want them to immediately understand what you do. Your key message must hit them right between the eyes.

Some exhibitors use lots of headlines and bullet points that couldn't be read by someone even a metre away, never mind by someone five metres away. Small pictures and images are to be avoided, too.

Imagine you see a picture of a water pump on a stand. You would think they produced water pumps, but you're not sure as the writing underneath is too small to be legible. Anyway, you're not interested in water pumps - your interest is water filtration. So you walk past the Acme Water Filtration Company. Because they aren't explicit in their messaging and don't drive home what they are selling and the benefits of their products.

Lots of exhibitors make the mistake of trying to say too much: they want the attendees to know everything they can do, but the result is that no one finds out what they do as there is too much information to take in.

Stand Design: Shell Scheme

If you book a pre-built shell scheme, you will get some wall panels that define your space, some carpet and a name plate above your stand. The rest is up to you - you will have to transform the bland walls before the exhibition starts. The exhibition manual will detail what you can and can't do with the shell scheme, so pay close attention to this to ensure your design doesn't break the rules or infringe health and safety regulations. If it does, the exhibition organisers will ask you to remove anything that doesn't comply.

You will be somewhat limited in terms of design on a stand like this, but there are still lots of ways to brand it and make it your own.

You could invest in some pop-up exhibition systems. These are self-contained units you can have designed with your images and key messages. They either roll up or pack into a case. All you do is unpack them and pop them up to give your stand an instant lift and brand look. They can be used again and again if you take care of them and the panels can be replaced if your key messages change or you want to focus on another message at a different exhibition

You could order furniture – chairs, tables, display racks, shelving - from the exhibition manual. But remember not to let a small stand become cluttered, leaving no space for visitors.

If you don't want to invest in a pop-up stand, consider ordering posters that you can affix to the walls of your stand with Velcro. Get them printed on foam board - they will be more robust and stand out against the background of the shell scheme.

Stand Design: Space Only

If you have booked space only, that is exactly what you will get: just space, no walls, no carpet. Most companies that take space only have a bespoke stand made for them by a specialist exhibition design and build company.

If you go for this option, it is important that you work closely with your supplier to make sure you get a stand that is right for you and will communicate your key marketing messages effectively. A stand design brief outlining what you want is essential. Give them a copy of the exhibition manual, too, to ensure the build conforms to the rules and regulations.

If you are going to attend more than one exhibition, tell the design company you want to be able to use the stand more than once and that you want them to store it for you between exhibitions. Otherwise, they will develop a stand for single use only.

Stand Design: Facilities
Order everything you need for your stand from the exhibition manual before the deadline – from furniture to an electricity supply for your stand. Be clear about where you want electricity points, water or internet connections, as they will be installed by the contractors before you arrive. Moving them can be costly.

If you want to do demonstrations and presentations, have them fully prepared and working before the exhibition. For example, if you are an IT company and want to showcase your software, assign a person to be responsible for it. If you want to network computers and wireless isn't an option, make sure you take the right cables or supply them to your exhibition company before the event so they can be laid under the floor before the stand is built. It will be difficult to move them once the stand is up.

Lead Capture
Decide how you will record and categorise visitors to your stand. Most exhibitions offer a pen or swipe system that enables you to swipe a barcode on a visitor's exhibition badge and download the visitor's information into a database for your use. You can usually add some codes of your own such as:

1 = Hot lead	A = Product 1
2 = Warm lead	B = Product 2
3 = Lukewarm lead	C = Service 1
4 = Cold lead	D = Service 2

This enables you to prioritise the people to follow up after the exhibition. The data can be downloaded into Excel or a database and you can start using it to follow up leads as soon as you get back to the office.

If you don't want to use an electronic system, use printed lead sheets that include:

- Contact details – name, company, job title, address, telephone and email. Staple business cards to the sheets to save time, but remember that not everyone remembers to bring business cards with them
- Their interest, products, services, challenges
- What type of lead? Use a number system like the one above to avoid writing down "hot lead" in front of your visitor

The information will have to be entered into Excel or your database, at the end of each day of the exhibition or as soon as you return to the office so that you can get in touch with visitors to your stand ASAP. Step 4 explains in more detail what to do with these leads.

Marketing Literature
The type of marketing literature you have available will depend on your goals for the exhibition. As a minimum, everyone from your company should take business cards, but do you really need to take 20 boxes of brochures? It might be better to take some guides or tip sheets that form part of your key message approach. Or you might not take anything except promotional items, so that you can speak to people individually, find out what they are really interested in, record it and send out the appropriate information after the exhibition.

Exhibition Promotions
When you have identified your objectives for the exhibition and what you want to communicate, think of creative ways to grab people's attention and get them to visit your stand. Don't just rely on giving away promotional items like pens, mugs and stress balls.

Think creatively. Use the ideas tool in *Chapter 5* to help you come up with ways to get your stand noticed. Ideas that work include:

- Use an entertainer or performer to entice people on to your stand. Mind-readers, magicians and fortune tellers are great, but they must have a connection to your overall theme - don't use them just for the sake of it.

- Give a presentation on a particular topic, and not one based solely on your products and services. Put up a poster explaining what visitors will learn from your presentation and detailing the times that it is taking place.

- Unusual promotional items capture the visitor's attention, something a little different from run-of-the-mill give-aways; something they will want to keep that reminds them of you and your company. During one of the hottest summers on record, we saw an ice-cream seller on a stand. To get a free ice-cream, visitors had to hand in their business cards. The exhibitors got a lot of business cards and more importantly had an opportunity to talk to people in the queue.

- Run a competition on your stand. Offer a worthwhile prize or prizes, not just a bottle of champagne, and relate it to your theme or marketing message.

- Refreshments. Offer tea, coffee and cold drinks on your stand to perk up tired visitors and encourage them to spend more time talking to you.

Exhibition Marketing

Although the organisers will be busy promoting the exhibition, they won't be focused on getting visitors to your stand. You will have to market yourself to the decision-makers who are likely to attend the show, before they come through the door. Here's how:

- Get included in the show catalogue with a good profile that gives your stand number and explains any promotions you are running.

- Add a flash to any adverts running in trade publications at least two months in advance telling readers what exhibition you are attending with your stand number.

- Get free exhibition tickets from the organisers to send to your clients and prospects inviting them to the exhibition and your stand. You could include an offer such as a free consultation at the show – ask them to call and book or register on your website.

- Advertise or offer to write an article to be sent to visitors before the show. Do the same for the exhibition catalogue which is given to all visitors as they enter the show.

- Ask about sponsorship or speaking opportunities at the exhibition. Find out how you can get involved in any pre-show activities. Get to know your key contact. Organisers will often allow the inclusion of some marketing material in packs they send out to people who pre-register - find out if you can include information about your company, product launch or show promotion.

- Your website should highlight your attendance and have a link to register for the show.

- Create some press releases and a press pack to leave in the press room at the show. Contact journalists to find out if they will be at the exhibition and ask if you can meet them there.

Pre-Show Briefing
Regardless of the size of your stand, it is essential to brief everyone representing your company. At least two weeks before the show, you should:

- Appoint a stand manager (it could be you) who will be responsible for running the stand during the show and be the main contact.

- Choose who is going to attend from your company. Nominate employees who are friendly and personable and used to dealing with clients. Consider including some technical experts who could help out with specialist knowledge.

- Have a rota. This is especially important if you have a large stand - you need to know who will be on the stand each day and what their responsibilities are. Build in coffee breaks and lunch breaks so that no one gets hungry, tired or jaded, and ensure there is always someone on the stand.

- Confirm that each nominated employee can attend and book their overnight accommodation and travel, if required.

- Give specific instructions about their roles, when you expect them on the stand, where they are staying, how to get to the exhibition venue, and most importantly give them their exhibition passes. .

- Ensure everyone knows the key theme, what you want to communicate during the show and the type of leads you are looking for. Remember, they don't have to sell products or services at the show, just make contacts and find out more about what visitors are looking for.

- Show the team any promotional items and literature you will be handing out at the exhibition.

- If you are demonstrating a product, make sure everyone on the stand can run a demonstration, or knows the people responsible, and that they have at least a working knowledge of your products and services.

Exhibition Planning

You must have a detailed plan or deadline checklist outlining what needs to be done, when and by whom. This will make sure that your exhibition plans stay on track and ensures that you stay in control of the process and your exhibition is a success.

Step 3 – At The Exhibition

Before The Exhibition

Whether you have a large stand or a shell scheme, be there to oversee the build and to ensure the stand looks as good as possible. It is a good idea to be there to handle any problems, like missing electrics or furniture, before visitors and your employees arrive. It is also an opportunity to organise any marketing literature, store any promotional items and check that all technical presentations or demos are working.

Sometimes getting everything organised can lead to a late night, but it means that on the morning of the first day of the exhibition everything will be perfect and you will be ready to promote your company.

Build-up days are usually one to three days before the exhibition. You will be notified about when you can access your stand or when your exhibition company can start building.

Morning Briefings
Gather everyone on the stand at least 30 minutes before the exhibition opens, each day of the show. Go over the day's roster and breaks. Demonstrate the use of the lead capture pen or swipe if you have one, or put someone in charge of using it. Make sure everyone knows what their role is and is familiar with the system for collecting leads. They should be enthusiastic and proactive so that they will encourage people to come on to the stand and talk to them. Employees should never be seen gathered at the back of the stand chatting among themselves, looking bored or just staring into space.

The Exhibition
Your stand looks great, your people have been briefed and know what to do, your promotional items are ready - all you need are visitors. An enticing stand will do some of the hard work for you and attract visitors to the stand. Some people will need a little more encouragement from your team.

Give your visitors time to take a look around before you approach them. Remember, this is not a hard sell. Just chat to them, find out what they are looking for and how you might be able to help. When you know more, offer them a demonstration, guide or information and, most importantly, record their details, especially their level of interest and the products that interest them. Hundreds of people could visit your stand - it will be impossible to remember what each one was interested in.

At the end of Day 1, tidy the stand and get everything ready for the following day – it will be one less thing to do in the morning. If your stand is due to be cleaned, you may want to confirm with the exhibition office that it is being done.

Download the leads for the day and email them back to the office if you have a pen or swipe system. If you have paper leads, enter them on a laptop and email them back to the office – this means you won't have to face inputting up to three days' worth of leads at the end of the exhibition.

Finally, if you and your team are staying overnight, wind down and relax. Don't drink too much and avoid spicy or garlic-laden food: a stand full of people with hangovers who smell of alcohol and garlic is not an appealing proposition. It is surprising how many exhibitors throw themselves into the nights out at an exhibition rather than focus on why they are there.

Exhibition Break-Down

You will be given a time when you can start breaking down your stand - you will not be allowed to do it before this time. If you want to get away promptly, ask someone else to go out early and drive the van or car to the loading area queue. At some exhibitions, loading space is limited and opens at a set time. If you leave it too late, you could be at the wrong end of a very long queue.

If you have had a stand built, make sure your contractors are there on time to break it down. Check that you take everything that needs to go back to your office in your vehicle. Don't rely on the exhibition company to identify your belongings and return them.

If you have a shell scheme or have rented any furniture, etc, make sure the rental company collects it and provides confirmation that they have picked it up. If you leave without doing this, you could be liable for a fine if they are unable to locate the equipment.

Re-Booking

Exhibition organisers will usually make an appointment with you towards the end of the show to talk about re-booking your stand and location for the following year. They usually require a deposit to secure your space, payable at the time or a few days later.

Unless you are absolutely certain the exhibition has been a resounding success, don't sign on the dotted line. You will want to follow up the leads the exhibition has generated to see if they will yield sales before committing yourself to the following year's event.

They do not re-book all the stands at the end of an exhibition; you will always be able to get a good space days, or even weeks, later. They may offer a discount if you book on the day, but it won't be such a great deal once you realise the exhibition didn't yield strong results. If you re-book then cancel, you will probably lose your deposit. Don't be pressurised into re-booking.

Step 4 – After The Exhibition

As with other marketing activities, follow-up is very important after an exhibition.

If you followed our advice about categorising the leads, you will be able to identify the hottest down to those who expressed a vague interest. Follow up the hottest leads first - as soon as you can. It is usually best to call them to find out more about the issues you discussed on the stand and how you can help them.

Work through the list of hot and warm prospects immediately after the exhibition and make appointments to see them or send them further information.

While you are calling the hotter leads, write to the lukewarm and cold ones to thank them for visiting the stand. Include further information if appropriate and invite them to contact you for a guide or audit. Although they don't currently need your products or services, they may want them in the future, so don't dismiss them. Add them to your contact database and include them in regular ongoing marketing activity.

COLD CALLING – PLENTY OF OTHER THINGS TO DO FIRST

There are easier ways of generating interest in your company than hammering the phones day after day trying to find individuals interested in your products and services.

Calling prospects to find out if they want to buy from you can bring results, but it can be hard work and, as we outlined in *Chapter 3*, it can be compared to your doctor calling you to find out if you have an ear infection and need antibiotics.

You can bet that if your doctor called 100 patients she might hit on one or two who did need antibiotics, but it would take a long time to find them and she would have made 98 wasted calls in between times.

We're not suggesting you shouldn't do cold calling, just that you should evaluate the effort required against the results you can achieve. Think about how you feel when you get a cold call from someone you have never spoken to you before. Unless they quickly get across what they want to communicate to you and it connects with you, as you have a real need at that time for what they are offering, you can't get them off the phone quickly enough.

Look at other methods of marketing: setting yourself up as an expert and getting people to come to you through speaking opportunities; networking; precisely focused direct mail; or optimising your website. If you use these methods and someone approaches you, you know they have a challenge, issue or problem they want your help with. Isn't that a better position to be in than making phone call after phone call and hoping you get lucky and find someone who needs your services?

Cold calling has its place but it should not be your main marketing activity. If you want to call a bunch of people you have never spoken to before to find out if they want your products and services, go ahead. You might consider working with a professional telemarketing agency that is practiced at cold calling and getting to decision-makers. However, for the telemarketing to succeed, you still need a good marketing system that can support requests for information and follow-up meetings. And you still need a good website, effective company literature and strong messaging.

SPONSORSHIP

Sponsorship is not just for the big consumer brands like Coca Cola and Virgin. It can work in the B2B world, too, and is a good way to raise awareness of your products and services. Sponsorship opportunities come in many shapes and sizes, from golf days to business dinners and awards ceremonies. However, it can be expensive and, as with all the marketing activities we have covered, you must be clear about why you want to do it and what you hope to achieve.

If you are seeking sponsorship for an event or in a publication, you could also use this checklist to ensure you are developing an attractive sponsorship package that will attract potential clients. This can be very important, especially if you have never sponsored anything before. You must clearly outline the benefits of sponsorship and demonstrate what can be achieved.

The Checklist

Use this checklist to find out if sponsorship is for you and how you could benefit from it:

- ☐ **Analyse the situation.** Look at other businesses that are sponsoring in your target market. Are competitors already doing this? Is it giving them with an advantage?
- ☐ **Be proactive.** Look for opportunities to sponsor events or publications that your target market will attend or read, e.g., charity events, your local Chamber of Commerce, Rotary Club events, specialist supplements in trade magazines. Sometimes it is more effective to focus your sponsorship efforts on one or two companies that attract your target audience than to seek numerous opportunities.
- ☐ **Define the sponsorship objectives.** Do you want to raise awareness of the brand, build an image, or promote a new product? What do you want to achieve by sponsorship?
- ☐ **Timescale.** Will it be a one-off event or a longer-term sponsorship package such as a series of networking events, or a range of events and publications over a longer period?

☐ **Does the sponsorship make sense?** Does it fit with any other promotional activities you are doing? Can one activity benefit from the other? E.g. what press coverage can you expect?

☐ **What's included?** Ensure you fully understand what the sponsorship package includes: what you will be responsible for and what the company you are sponsoring will be responsible for. More importantly, be sure you have the resources, time and money to make the most of the sponsorship before agreeing to it. Consider negotiating the following entitlements before you commit:

  o Exclusivity within your industry
  o Supply of tickets/admittance for you and, say, ten guests to each event
  o Provision of database of attendees or members of an organisation with the right to market to them. Check they have the right to pass on this information under data protection laws
  o Display of banners and promotional materials at the events you are sponsoring
  o Scope to make and present awards
  o Inclusion of adverts in magazines or communications sent to their members or target audience
  o Opportunities to write articles if you are sponsoring a guide or supplement
  o Recognition of your sponsorship at all events, with an opportunity to address the audience
  o Links from their website to your website and inclusion of information about your company in their newsletters or ezines
  o Joint press releases that promote the events to secure press coverage

☐ The cost should not exceed the benefits or eat into your budget by using money you could spend on something else, especially if you want lots of leads.

- ☐ The initial investment in sponsorship is only half the cost. If you sponsor a series of events, you will have to host each one, develop marketing literature and invite key clients or prospects to attend.
- ☐ Work with the organisation you are sponsoring and get creative: think of fun or different ways to sponsor an event to cut through all the other things that might go on and get yourselves noticed.
- ☐ Agree sponsorship success criteria and include it any agreement you sign. If the sponsorship doesn't deliver the results you agreed, you can pull out of the contract with no penalties.
- ☐ If the sponsorship is for a large sum of money, ask if you can pay in instalments.

MARKETING LITERATURE – WHAT DO YOU REALLY NEED?

With the proliferation of information on the internet, do you really need to produce reams of marketing literature to support your marketing campaigns and sales efforts? Isn't your website enough? The answer is that printed material is still important, but you should proceed with caution and think hard about what needs to be printed and what can be produced as e-literature for people to print if they choose. This chapter looks at the many types of marketing literature you could produce, all of which could be produced as e-literature or printed.

Guides & White Papers

In *Chapter 3* we outlined how important it is for you to set yourself up as an expert in your particular sector to demonstrate to potential clients that you are an authority on a subject area.

One of the easiest ways to do this is to write a guide or "white paper" on a subject you know inside out and would be of interest to your clients and potential clients. Write it with them in mind. The content should relate to something specific and the document should contain valuable information and have an interesting title, such as:

- How to Generate Sales Leads Through Internet Marketing

- Top Ten Ways to Secure Your IT Network
- Insider Tips on Developing Business Property
- 20 Ways to Increase Your Profitability
- The IR 35 Rule Explained
- 100 Tips for Stressed-out IT Managers
- How to Create Successful Direct Mail Campaigns
- Marketing Inspirations
- Manual Handling – The Definitive Guide
- 87 Ways to Improve Your Sales Performance
- Six Steps to Six-Figure Profits
- Everything You Need to Know about Firewalls
- Manager's Guide to Listening Skills
- Little Known Ways to Develop Your Sale Pipeline

Choose a title that will interest your target market and get writing! It doesn't have to be expertly designed, as long as it is easy to read, has clear images and diagrams to explain concepts and provides the reader with useful information. Publish it as a PDF and start using it. There are lots of ways to use it, here are a few:

- Publish it on your website for download – ask for users' details if you want to know who is downloading it.
- Use it as a hook for a direct mail – Contact us for your FREE Guide to…
- Print and distribute to attendees at your next speaking engagement as a thank you for attending the event.
- Print and distribute it to delegates at your next exhibition or seminar.
- Send to prospective clients instead of, or as well as, the usual brochure – send it via email or print it and send by post.

Here is a simple approach to help you gather your thoughts about content:

1. Write down five to ten areas you want the guide to cover.
2. Under each heading, write an outline of what you want to cover - this could include a list of bullet points or key concepts.

3. Research each of the areas you want to cover and take a note of the quotes, industry statistics, innovations, rules or regulations you want to include under each heading.

4. Build your guide, chunk by chunk. Some of the most effective guides are only 12 pages long, so don't worry about making it any longer. It is more important that it conveys an impression of expertise and knowledge and provides the reader with vital information.

Include a call to action at the end of the guide. Let the reader know how you can help them overcome the challenges outlined in the guide and invite them to contact you. Include at least your telephone number, website address and email contact details. Consider directing them to your website where they can download more articles and guides.

Tip Sheets

Tip sheets are short versions of guides. Only one or two pages long, they give your target audience a taste of your knowledge and encourage them to think about their challenges and how you could help. They can be quick to produce and enable your target audience to pick up important titbits of information. Titles could include:

- Ten Reasons Why 70% of Start-Ups Fail
- 20 Ways to Ensure Marketing Success
- Proven Ways to Improve Your Sales Techniques
- Top Tips for HR Managers – Managing Stress
- 15 Ways to Improve your ROI on Commercial Property
- 20 Advertising Mistakes and How Not to Make Then
- IT Security Checklist
- 12 Reasons to Change Your IT Provider

As with guides, include a call to action and your contact details.

Articles

Articles sit somewhere between guides and tip sheets. They are usually two to four pages long and cover just one key subject area, whereas a guide may cover more than one subject area. Including them on your website can be very good for search engine optimisation (SEO) - you can submit articles for publication on sites that will link back to your site as the source. *Chapter 8* covers SEO in more detail, but two of the most popular article sites are: *www.ezinearticles.com* and *www.submityourarticle.com*

Brochures

Most businesses think they need a brochure but, if you have a great website and a good range of articles, guides and tip sheets, you may not need a brochure, too. Think, when you go to see a prospective client, what holds more value for them - a guide or a brochure? What are they more likely to read - a guide or a brochure?

Brochures have their place but they must be developed with your target audience in mind. We see many brochures that are written from the company's perspective: we do this, we do that, we are great at XYZ, we produce this. The prospective client doesn't get a look in if the company is too busy shouting about what it does.

If you decide you do need a company brochure to support your marketing efforts, write it with the prospective client at the forefront of your mind. Think about what they need to know about your company, what challenges they may be facing and how you can help them.

Help yourself by doing the exercise in *Chapter 3* which encourages you to think like your clients and understand what drives them to buy. Also, think about whether the content in the brochure answers these five questions:

1. Why would the prospect want to read what you have written?
2. Why should they believe what you have to say?
3. Why should they do anything about what you are offering?
4. Why should they act now?
5. What are the three key things you must communicate?

The "less is more rule" comes into play when creating a brochure. Use images or diagrams to get across complex services or products so that the reader can quickly assimilate how your product works or how your products work together. You don't have to tell the prospective client everything - if you do, they won't read it all. Minimise the amount of words you use and just communicate key pieces of information.

Work with a designer who is experienced in drafting brochures and understands how to use images and typography to good effect. Supply a good brief, like the one outlined below. This will give them an understanding of what you want to communicate and the look and feel you want to achieve.

Brochure Brief

WHAT IS THE FOCUS
What do you want to achieve with the brochure?
TARGET AUDIENCE
Who is the brochure targeted at? What does the target audience currently know about us?
CURRENT PERCEPTIONS
How is our company currently perceived in the marketplace? What does the target audience know about our products and services? What do they need to know about us?
PRODUCTS OR SERVICES OVERVIEW
What is our current product/service range? What are the key benefits or our products/services?
WHAT ARE THE COMPELLING REASONS TO BUY?
What the emotional drivers and challenges our clients face?
PROPOSITION
How can the target audience benefit from our products or services? Why should they respond to the brochure – what is the call to action?
TONE
Is there a tone of voice or personality/image we need to maintain, enhance, replace or create?
GUIDELINES/MANDATORY INCLUSIONS
Are there any legal or product-related inclusions we need to consider? What logos/brands imagery (people and products) must be included?
TIMESCALES
What are the timescales?
ADDITIONAL COMMENTS
Print quantity, quality of paper, types of printing finish, etc.

Folder

The requirement for a folder depends on the type of products or services you sell. If you regularly send out quotes or proposals, consider creating a branded folder into which you can insert information and documentation. Also, consider combining a brochure and folder so that you can provide details about your company on the first few pages and insert more detailed information and a business card in a folder pocket at the back.

If you decide to produce a folder, do some checks before you commission a design and print.

- Assess the thickness of the paper you use for the proposals and quotes you send out – the pocket will have to be designed to accommodate the documents you want to include and hold them securely.
- Place holders or slots on the folder must be the correct size so that your business cards fit neatly, without bending or falling out.

If you don't really need a folder, produce a branded proposal cover that will make your quotes and proposals stand out and give a professional look to your communication with clients and prospects.

Case Studies

Case studies are a powerful way of communicating your expertise, knowledge and the way you work with your clients. It is important to build up a portfolio of customer success stories that highlight different aspects of your products and services and demonstrate how you have helped clients address their challenges.

Case studies show you have implemented real-life solutions that were so successful the company you worked with is happy to endorse its relationship with you. They are also great for PR if you can get a trade publication to run the story. However, you must always have the permission of the client to use their case study and they must always be given a copy of it and sign an agreement about how it is to be used.

To develop an effective and successful case study with content that works, there are some key questions to ask your client. But, do it in person or over the telephone - don't just send them a list of questions and expect them to answer them. You will wait a long time to get what you want. It is easier for the client to answer your questions verbally and you will get more of the type of information you want from them.

- Can they supply a company overview and a few more words about their company's current strengths?

- What challenges did they face before using your company? What issues were irritating them? Why did they feel they needed a new solution?

- What were the project goals? What did they want to achieve by working with you or buying your product or service?

- What did your product or service enable them to do that they weren't able to do before? What was the main improvement they gained as a result of working with you?

- Why did they select your company, product or service?

- What was particularly successful about the partnership or can they identify one thing that stood out for them?

Once you have all this information, you can produce your case study using a simple structure we devised that keeps the case study focused and easy to read. You don't have to produce pages of information: just one or two pages that give prospective clients an overview of what working with you would be like and some relevant pictures.

- **The company** – Include a paragraph about the company, what it does and its strengths in the marketplace.

- **The challenge** – Outline the challenges the company faced or the issues it wanted to overcome. Be careful not to make the client look incompetent or useless. Highlight why you were selected to help.

- **The solution** – Show how your product or service helped address the challenges and how the project was implemented. Some information may be sensitive, so don't go into lots of detail, just cover the main points.

- **The quote** – Ask the client for a quote, be specific and ask what they thought was particularly successful about the project or what positive changes your product or service made to the company.

Publish case studies on your website, have them printed for marketing purposes and, where appropriate, get PR coverage in trade publications.

Information or Datasheets

Information or datasheets have traditionally been used in business-to-business marketing to provide specific information about individual products or services. They tend to include "dry" information about a product or service, reference to its features and, if it is IT-based, screen shots to show how the software works.

These are useful pieces of marketing literature as they provide focused information on a particular product or service that may not be included in a brochure or other marketing material. They can be created as PDF documents and included on your website for download or they can be printed and given to prospective clients who want more detailed information on a certain product or service in your range.

However, care should be taken to make datasheets informative and interesting to read, giving the reader more than just basic facts about the product. If they are boring or don't connect with your target audience, they won't be read.

Here are some headings you can use on your information or datasheets that will help you communicate the benefits and structure the information in a logical way.

- **Overview.** Tell them what does the product or service does and what key challenges or problems it overcomes.
- **What will Acme Product do for you?** Tell them what the product or service will do for them, what benefits they can expect as a result of using it.
- **What makes Acme Product different?** Tell them what makes your product or service different, what makes you stand out from the competition.
- **Why Choose Acme Corp?** Outline what makes your company a good choice from which to buy this particular product or service.
- **What are your next steps?** Guide the reader and tell them want to do: visit your website, call you for a free guide or audit, or contact you for more detailed information.

Technical Notes

If you work in a technical industry such as engineering, IT or manufacturing, you should consider producing technical notes. This type of information should give the reader an in-depth overview of the product or service and include important data such as transfer speeds, tolerances, measurements, etc.

Technical notes are distinct from information or datasheets. They cover hardcore data, the inside leg measurement on your products and services, if you will. This is the type of information you should make available only to those who ask for it or seek it out. If you use it as general marketing literature, it can put off or confuse buyers if they don't have the technical knowledge they need to understand and interpret this level of information.

What you put in your technical notes is up to you, but even at this level of detail, the content should be broken down into headings and be easy to read; technical data should be presented in tables or diagrams.

Promotional Items

Promotional items are a good way of keeping your brand in the minds of your clients and prospective clients. They won't deliver sales leads to your door in an instant, but if you choose your promotional items wisely, your brand will at least be in your prospects' line of vision.

There are thousands of promotional items to choose from: USB sticks, mugs, pens, Post-it notes, diaries, notepads, paper weights - the list is endless. We recommend choosing items your target audience will use in the office, or as part of their job, on a regular basis. We use branded Post-it notes, pads, pens and mugs and we give a set to each prospective client we visit. They are not the most innovative products, but all the items are useful - they will write on the Post-it notes, use the pen and pad and drink from the mug. Our brand will be in front of them for at least the next few weeks and will prompt them to think about us more than they would if they had received nothing at all.

If you want to be more innovative, particularly if you work in the IT industry and want to give your target audience the latest storage device or technical device branded with your logo, make sure it is something they are likely to use.

Include your telephone number and/or your website address on the promotional item, making it easy for them to contact you. If they are using your pen to work round ideas to solve a problem, you want them to call you there and then, not to have to go and look up your contact details.

Marketing Literature Review

Before you commission a designer and start writing content for your marketing literature, use this simple checklist to decide what items to produce and whether to have them printed, created just as PDFs, or both.

ITEM	REQUIRED	PRINTED	PDF
Guides/White Papers	❑	❑	❑
Tip Sheets	❑	❑	❑
Articles	❑	❑	❑
Brochure	❑	❑	❑
Folder	❑	❑	-
Proposal front cover	❑	❑	-
Case Studies	❑	❑	❑
Info/datasheets	❑	❑	❑
Technical Notes	❑	❑	❑
Promotional Items	❑	-	-

PRESENTATIONS – OR DEATH BY POWERPOINT

Marketing presentations that promote your company are now an accepted way of presenting information. However, many presentations are dull, uninspiring, talk about the company, not what you can do for the client, and contain so many bullet points that the audience are dying of boredom by the end. You are likely to have sat through at least one of these in the last six months. We bet you couldn't wait for it to end. Wouldn't it be awful if you were making the same impression on your perspective clients?

What can you do to ensure your presentations have impact? The first step is to decide whether you actually need a PowerPoint presentation. In many cases, you don't.

We never do a PowerPoint presentation at a first meeting with a client. We take time to find out what they need, ask questions and listen to what they have to say. We don't make them listen to us. We are there to find out how we can help them, not to tell them how great our company is.

However, if you do need to deliver a PowerPoint presentation, whether for a client meeting, seminar or other event, here are some ways to make your presentation memorable for all the right reasons.

In '*The Jelly Effect - Making Your Communication Stick*', Andrew Bounds recommends a simple three-step method - RAP – to plan presentations:

1. Results – what do you want to achieve?
2. Audience – who are they, what do they want to learn?
3. Preparation – only start planning your presentation when you know what you want the results to be and who your audience is.

The graph on the next page shows what happens to the audience's concentration levels over time.

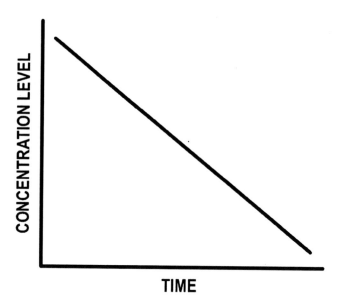

The audience's concentration level is highest in the first five to ten minutes of the presentation and reduces as time goes on. Presentations tend to follow a logical sequence, with some scene-setting and general company information first and the best bits about 20 or 30 minutes in. By then, concentration levels are reducing, and some people will have stopped listening.

- You should get your most important information across in the first few slides. Don't leave the best till last, especially in a sales presentation. Tell them what they need to know first off.

- Use images and diagrams to communicate key points. People remember pictures and recall them more effectively than words. For example, if a company wanted to convey the size and scope of its logistics plant, the presenter should use an aerial photo and highlight each of the key areas of the plant and what happens in each section. This is much more effective than a bulleted list of square footage statistics.

- Remember, what counts is what the audience remembers after the presentation and what they do with that information. A strong call to action at the end jolts their fading concentration and brings them back to what you wanted to achieve with the presentation.

- It is a cliché, but to fail to prepare is to prepare to fail. Be prepared: practise your presentation thoroughly, prepare cue cards to keep you in sync with your slides.
- For tips on creating PowerPoint presentations with impact, go to *www.m62.net*. This UK-based company specialises in developing powerful presentations. The site has some great resources on presentation theory with videos that show what works and what doesn't.

8. Making The Internet Work For You

"Almost overnight, the internet's gone from a technical wonder to a business must."
BILL SCHRADER

The internet is an incredible marketing tool. Using it means much more than hosting a simple website. It offers ways to communicate and interact with clients and potential clients that goes far beyond the written word. You can use images, video, audio, live online seminars, tele-calls, podcasts - the list goes on. Covering all the ways you can market your company on the internet would mean adding a few thousand more pages to this book. So we will stick to the areas we feel are truly useful in business-to-business marketing and, where applicable, provide links to useful resources that expand the subject area.

YOUR WEBSITE

Your website can be a powerful marketing tool, or it can just sit out there on the internet doing absolutely nothing for you, acting as an electronic version of your company brochure that your target audience will only ever find if you tell them the web address. We see hundreds of B2B websites languishing in the dark reaches of the internet that could be transformed with just a little bit of care and attention.

There are hundreds of decision-makers searching for information on the type of products and services you supply. If your website doesn't come to their attention, one of your competitors' sites will. You must do everything you can to make sure your website is out there paying its way, promoting you as the expert you are, delivering leads to your door and selling products for you.

WHAT DO YOU WANT TO ACHIEVE?

How can you make sure your website does its job? There are thousands of web designers, search engine optimisation companies, Google Pay-per-Click companies and internet advertising agencies all offering to make your website the coolest, best performer in Google searches or the best designed. The choice can be overwhelming, but this isn't where to start. You start, as with most of the marketing activities covered in this book, with:

"What do you want your website to do for your company?"

Do you want to generate leads, sell products, look great, demonstrate your knowledge, or build a community? Perhaps it's a combination of these. What you want from your site will shape the approach or technology you use to create it.

Write down what you want your website to do for you. Make the list as long or short as you want, but cover everything:

SITE MAP – KEY TO STRUCTURE AND CONTENT

When you know what you want from your website, think about the type of information you want to provide through it, what you want to communicate or sell to visitors and how it will be structured.

If you already have a website, you could use it as a basis for a revamped site, but sometimes it is easier to start from scratch. This gives you an opportunity to really consider what you want your website to do. A good way to do this is to develop a map of your website that enables you to visualise the content and structure and gives you an overview of its size and depth.

This simple example is the map of a site for a company that sells widgets:

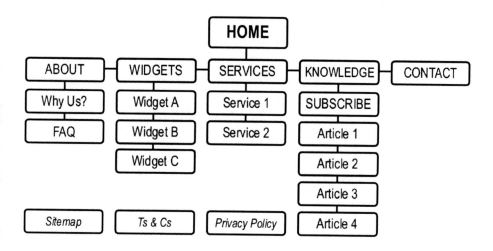

IT'S NOT JUST ABOUT DESIGN

There is more to creating your website than producing something that looks good. If you want a site that ranks highly on Google and other search engines, converts visitors into paying customers or delivers quality enquiries, you need to develop a web strategy that will turn your website into a powerful marketing magnet.

You will need to focus on a number of areas to ensure your website delivers the type of visitors that you want. These include:

- **Content** – Google and other search engines love relevant content. The more you have and the more regularly you add to it, the better your chances of securing a higher ranking on Google.

- **Types of content** – Don't just rely on words - use video and audio files to bring your site alive and talk to visitors. Google likes video content and this can also help the rankings of your website.

- **Keywords** – Using relevant keywords throughout your website is essential. Gone are the days when you could "trick" search engines by hiding lots of keywords in your site. Google and other engines are looking for relevancy, how often a keyword appears and how it relates to other keywords in your site.

- **Design** – The design of your website must encourage visitors to take action. There are lots of things you can do to ensure certain items are placed in key positions that will encourage visitors to click through.

- **Website code** – The code behind your website is also relevant. If there is too much javascript or cluttered programming, the search engine spiders that come to check out your site won't be able to find the content they are looking for and will either index your site incorrectly or just give up.

SEARCH ENGINE OPTIMISATION (SEO) – WHAT REALLY WORKS!

When you search on Google, results are returned as two lists. The following screenshot shows the information that was returned when we searched for "computer security products":

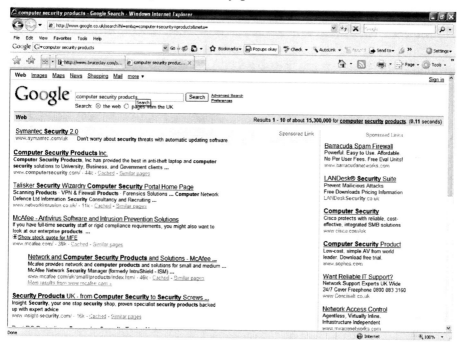

The results beginning on the second listing on the left are organic, or natural, results from websites focused on specific keywords and relevant content. The results along the top and on the right, highlighted along with the words "Sponsored Link(s)", are Pay-Per-Click (PPC) adverts.

This section helps you to increase your organic Search Engine Ranking Position (SERP) but later in this chapter we'll deal with PPC advertising too. Our aim is to give you the basics on SERP and to help you understand it, with links to more detailed information if you want to find out more.

Beware! There are no guarantees with search engine optimisation, but there are hundreds of companies that will take your money for a service that will guarantee a quick and easy front-page ranking on Google. This may have been possible a few years ago, but the search engines are getting smarter and smarter. So, choose your agency wisely and take up references.

No one except Google really knows how their algorithm for ranking websites works - it is a closely guarded secret. They released Patent Number 20050071741 on "Information Retrieval Based on Historical Data", in other words, their search page results. The document included more than 100 factors and calculations that affect a website's position in the search engine rankings. If you want to read it, you will find it on the US Patent and Trademark Office website, *www.uspto.gov*. If you want to read a good review of how it can be interpreted, visit the SEO blog at:
www.seomoz.org/article/google-historical-data-patent

Getting good rankings on Google doesn't happen overnight. If your site isn't optimised right now, it could take a few months for your SEO efforts to take effect. If you want prospective clients to visit your site immediately, consider taking PPC adverts on Google or MSN. You can set up adverts in a day and have people clicking through to your site within hours.

Google

Why focus your efforts on Google? There are other search engines out there. The fact is that 90% of all searches undertaken on the web are through Google. According to market analysts ComScore, 37.1 billion searches were conducted using Google sites in August 2007. It makes sense to try to get your website ranked on Google, particularly in the B2B world, as this is the search engine most businesses use, too.

OK, so the algorithm that Google use to rank your website is almost impossible to understand and they keep making minor changes to it, so how can we give you any advice on SERP? The answer is that there are some established factors that do make a difference to how your page is indexed and ranked by Google. We discuss them in the following sections.

SEARCH ENGINE OPTIMISATION – CONTENT & KEYWORDS ARE KING

The content of your website is highly important - when someone keys in a search term, Google looks at it and tries to match it with the websites that are indexed in its database. It develops this database using a Googlebot, a crawler or spider that comes to your website, tries to follow every link on your site and downloads and indexes as many pages as it can. It regularly sends a "freshbot" back to check if you have any new content and downloads and indexes that to the database, too. Fresh pages must be linked to and from other known pages on your website in order to be crawled and indexed to check you aren't putting up random pages. It is important to keep uploading fresh content to your website as this will ensure it is regularly visited by Google.

Once your website has been crawled and if the keywords and general content of your website match the search terms, Google will return your website or webpage(s) as a result. Just one problem - there will probably be a few thousand other companies trying to do the same thing. At the start of this chapter when we searched for "computer security products", Google returned over 15 million results! Therefore to optimise your site for this key phrase would be very difficult.

It is vital that you identify what keywords your decision-makers search on when they are looking for the products and services you provide. And you should research the keywords that will be most effective in helping your site move up the Google rankings.

How do you do this? It is not an exact science, and there is a plethora of information out there on the best way of doing it. If you want to read more about the subject, the following resources are reputable and always current.

www.google.com/webmasters/tools - Google have developed a website that gives guidance on how to build a Google-friendly website. There is a range of information, including tools to rank your current website and articles on how to optimise your website with keywords, etc.

www.searchengineguide.com - A useful website with information and tips for beginners, especially on keywords.

www.searchengineworkshops.com/seo-tip-of-the-day.html - John Alexander's website – he's a great guy who knows a lot about SEO. You can sign up for his "tip a day" email which has good information about keywords and other SEO tactics.

www.seobook.com – A good site developed by Arron Matthew Wall that provides lots of free SEO resources and PPC information. He has included lots of SEO tools, *http://tools.seobook.com*, that enable you to check how your website is ranked, etc.

These websites give detailed information on the importance of keywords. To make things easier for you, we have outlined some of the main areas you should think about when developing content and keywords for your site.

Finding The Right Keywords

It is tempting to think you can select just a few keywords that relate to your business, put them on your website and, hey presto! You will jump to the top of Google. Sadly, it doesn't work quite like that - as we showed above, searching for "computer security products" returned over 15 million results. A more focused effort is required if you want to win at the Google game.

The key (pardon the pun) to determining the best keywords for your website lies in finding a niche or specialist areas that other companies may not be focusing on, and thinking about what words people type into Google when they are looking for your products or services. By doing this, you won't be fighting to get ahead of the millions of other search results for the standard keywords.

So how do you get started?

Your Focus

First, think about what you are actually selling and who is your target market.

For example, if you are a business consultancy specialising in the engineering and manufacturing industries and have developed a unique business coaching service, there is no point trying to optimise your site for general "business consultancy". Firstly, you will be among thousands of companies trying to do the same, and, secondly, you won't attract your target market of engineering and manufacturing companies that are really interested in finding you.

Focus your efforts in the areas where you specialise or have a niche – this will improve your chances of being ranked in a high position on Google. Then develop a content and keyword strategy that will help to achieve this.

Keywords Vs Key Phrases

There is an important distinction between keywords and key phrases. A keyword is a single word; key phrases are predominantly what people actually type into search engines. For example, if you were looking for a marketing company you might type in:

> *"Marketing"*

However, it is more likely you will narrow this down to one of these key phrases or questions:

> *"Marketing company in Boston"*
>
> *"B2B marketing company"*
>
> *"Marketing company in London"*
>
> *"How do I find a good marketing company?"*
>
> *"Internet marketing company in Edinburgh"*

Think about what you type into search engines. It isn't normally one word; you want specific results, so you use a phrase or series of phrases until you get the kind of results you want.

The same is true for the decision-makers looking for your products and services; they want a solution to their problem and to get accurate results they will keep refining their search until they find what they are looking for.

Content and Keyword Strategy

Research and campaign planning are crucial if you are to achieve a better ranking on Google. Start by developing a site map like the example earlier in this chapter. Do this first - it will give you the structure you need to develop both your content and keyword strategy.

When the Googlebot indexes your site, it looks at a huge range of things – more than 100 calculations, according to Google's patent. However, we know that one of the things it does is look at your site as a whole to try to determine how relevant the content is. For example, if you had a website selling Christmas decorations, it would look for related content with words such as crackers, baubles, angels, bunting, tinsel, advent calendars, advent candles, Father Christmas, Santa Claus and Christmas lights, appearing throughout your site. It would look at the density of the keywords to find out if there were too many, i.e. if you were hiding keywords to try to rig the results, which it would penalise you for. Or, if it couldn't find enough keywords or relevancy so that it didn't believe that your site really did sell Christmas decorations, it would give it a lower ranking.

You should look at each page on your website, optimise its content and check its relevancy to other pages on your site. Take care when deciding which keywords and key phrases to include in your copy and in the code that search engines scan to enable them to understand what your site is all about.

Within the HTML code that drives how a website looks, there are areas called meta tags. These, along with the content of your website, help the search engines to "read" your website.

Meta titles, meta descriptions and meta keywords tags are used to carry great weight and could make the difference between a high and low ranking on Google. They have become less important in recent years, but you should still complete these tags as they affect how your website is displayed when a search is run on Google.

For example, when we searched Google for "brighter marketing" it returned these results:

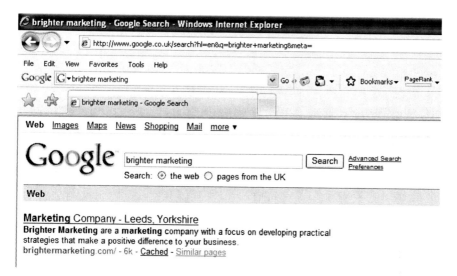

The first line (underlined link) will always display your **meta title** and the text below it will always display your **meta description**. If the search engine spider can't find these, it will search for the next available section of body text. The HTML code for our website demonstrates how the search engine returned what we wanted it to, not the first piece of text it found on the website.

```
<!DOCTYPE html
  PUBLIC "-//W3C//DTD XHTML 1.0 Strict//EN"
  "http://www.w3.org/TR/xhtml1/DTD/xhtml1-strict.dtd">
<html lang="en" xml:lang="en" xmlns="http://www.w3.org/1999/xhtml">
<head>
  <meta content="text/html; charset=utf-8" http-equiv="content-type" />
  <title>Marketing Company - Leeds, Yorkshire</title>
  <meta content="Brighter Marketing are a marketing company with a focus on developing practical strategies
that make a positive difference to your business." name="description" />
  <meta content="marketing agency company strategy consultancy design yorkshire, sheffield, leeds,
manchester, brighter marketing, brightermarketing" name="keywords" />
  <link media="all" href="/assets/styles/main.css" type="text/css" rel="stylesheet" />
  <link href="/favicon.ico" type="image/x-icon" rel="icon" />
```

So, when planning the content for your website, include a different title and meta description for each page that accurately reflects what that page is about. In this way, when your page gets indexed by Google, it will display the content you want it to.

How do you know which keywords and phrases will deliver a high ranking on Google? It is not an exact science and in some cases it just takes time and some research to understand what search terms are being used by people looking for your products and services.

For example, if we optimised our home page for the keyword "marketing", it would be difficult for us to rank highly on Google as the search term "marketing" returns over 7,000,000 results. However, a bit of research could tell us which search terms connected with our business returned fewer results.

To help you understand what you are searching for you could use Wordtracker, *www.wordtracker.com* to find out how many people are entering a particular search term and to see how effective it is.

Their free version, *http://freekeywords.wordtracker.com*, reveals how many searches for a particular keyword are undertaken on a daily basis and creates a list of related keywords. However, as great as this free tool is, it doesn't give you the intelligence you need to ensure you select high-ranking keywords and phrases for your site.

The full paid-for version is much more comprehensive and will do searches for both google.co.uk and google.com. Here is an example of what it can do.

If you search for a phrase such as "business coaching" and select Google.co.uk only, it will return all the search terms containing the words "business coaching". It brought back 184 results but we are showing only the top few:

Your UK keyword list

Keyword	Searches
business coaching	648
business coaching life	142
uk business coaching and mentoring	113
business coaching uk	101
executive business coaching	69
coaching business training	61
CIPD business coaching online magazine	55
coaching business	52
coaching in business opinion poll survey	51
cipd business coaching	50

This is great, and you might think that by using the keywords "business coaching" or "business coaching life" on your website, you will get to the top of Google. However, this is only half the story. You need to know how effective that keyword is, so you need to run an evaluation that will give you a Keyword Effectiveness Index or KEI. This is the formula that looks at how popular a keyword is against the results it returns in Google.

If there were 648 searches for "business coaching" in the last month but there were over a million results, it is likely the KEI would be very low.

Your UK keyword list

select ▾   delete ▾   save ▾   1 ▾ ▶

Keyword	Searches ▾	Google UK	Google UK KEI
business coaching	648	1,190,000	0.35
business coaching life	142	1,610	12.52
uk business coaching and mentoring	113	3	4,256.00
business coaching uk	101	1,890	5.40
executive business coaching	69	1,500	3.17
coaching business training	61	340	10.94
CIPD business coaching online magazine	55	0	–
coaching business	52	43,700	0.06
coaching in business opinion poll survey	51	0	–
cipd business coaching	50	0	–

As these results show, the KEI for "business coaching" is very low at only 0.35. As a rule, an effective keyword is one that has a KEI of over 100. You can see that "uk business coaching and mentoring" might be a good key phrase: there were 113 searches but only three search results were returned on Google.

To get a better view, you can sort by the highest KEI, which would give the following result:

Your UK keyword list

select ▾   delete ▾   save ▾   1 ▾ ▶

Keyword	Searches	Google UK	Google UK KEI ▾
uk business coaching and mentoring	113	3	4,256.00
business courses in coaching and mentoring	33	3	363.00
business training coaching mentoring seminars	18	1	324.00
business life coaching south east	24	2	288.00
business Coaching Devon	22	3	161.30
business leadership coaching south east	14	2	98.00
business professional life coaching	12	2	72.00
business executive coaching uk	9	2	40.50

You can use this to work out if any of those search phrases would be effective on your website. However, remember to always develop website copy for visitors to your site, not for search engines alone. The keywords and phrases you use must make sense in the copy and not be included just because they have a good KEI.

To check how well your website focuses on your client's needs and to ensure the copy makes sense to them, use *www.futurenowinc.com/wewe.htm*. It will provide an overview of any page on your website and gauge how focused your copy is on your client's needs.

Another useful feature of Keyword tracker is that it can tell you what keywords Google associates with "business coaching", enabling you to develop relevancy throughout your site. For example, the other top search terms associated with "business coaching" include "coach", "life coach", "executive coach", "development" and so on.

coaching

Why do I need related keywords? Click here

1. business coaching
2. business coach
3. executive coaching
4. corporate coaching
5. coach
6. coaching
7. business consulting
8. small business coaching
9. life coaching
10. Coach
11. business coaches
12. life coach
13. coaches
14. executive coach
15. success
16. management
17. entrepreneur
18. registered corporate coach
19. business
20. marketing
21. management coaching
22. professional coaching
23. consultant
24. Business Coach
25. small business coach
26. development

Now that you know what keywords and phrases to use, it is time to develop content for each page of your site. To ensure the best display results:

- The title tag should be no more than 70 characters long. If it is longer, Google will just cut it off in search results.

- The meta description should be no more than 120 characters long - again, any longer and Google will cut it off.

- Don't optimise for more than five keywords or phrases per page - more than this and Google might think you are trying to spam it.

- Overall, aim for a 10% keyword density on each page. Use this ratio if you don't know where to put your key words:

  number of paragraphs/number of keywords
  = number of keywords per paragraph

  To check this, use a keyword density checker, *www.webconfs.com/keyword-density-checker.php*, to give you an idea of how your keywords rank.

- The H1 tag is the title of your page that will be displayed in larger text at the top of your page and has some relevancy, so include at least one keyword or phrase.

Use the following approach as a basis for building the content for each of your pages. Take the pages in turn and work out the strategy for each one. This example could be used for the home page, but it is just as relevant to other pages on your site.

Meta Title: BMC Business Coaching Services – Amazing Results

Meta Description: Leading coaching services for stressed-out executives that deliver improved personal and work performance

Meta Keywords: business coaching, uk business coaching and mentoring, business professional life coaching, business executive coaching uk

H1 Tag: Get amazing results with our unique business coaching

Body Copy: We are the UK's leading business coaching company with a focus on improving the personal and professional lives of the people we work with...

To get a good idea of what a search engine spider sees when it visits your website, try one of the many simulators available, for example *www.iwebtool.com/spider_view*. It will give you an overview of how your SEO efforts are being interpreted by a search engine spider.

LINK POPULARITY

Keywords and key phrases are important when developing content for your website, but Google also ranks your site on the type and number of links it has, including internal links between pages and relevant content.

If you download the Google Toolbar (*http://toolbar.google.com*) you will see a green bar that ranks every site you visit on a scale of 1-10. Generally, sites with a page ranking of seven or more are considered excellent in terms of relevancy and popularity.

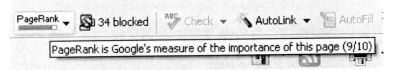

It appears the way Google calculates the relevancy of your web pages depends on the number of websites that link back to your site. However, you mustn't depend on just any old links: the sites you link to must also be of a good page ranking, relevancy and quality. Don't bother with link farms and other methods of generating links - the Googlebot won't be fooled. It is better to find links from sites and directories that have similar or related topics to yours and build these up over time, adding them month by month.

To find out how many sites are linking back to your site, type "link:www.yoursite.com" into the Google search bar. To find out how many sites were linked to Brighter Marketing, you would type "link:www.brightermarketing.com". This won't return all the back-links, but it will give you a good idea of how many are listed. You could do the same thing on Yahoo and MSN to get a fuller picture.

Don't worry if there aren't that many links: if you haven't been focused on acquiring them, you can't expect there to be a lot. However, a focused approach will help you to increase the number of links and to improve your page ranking.

How do you find sites that want to link to your site? You could use PR Prowler, a reputable piece of software that finds sites and directories for you to submit your details to. For around £50 ($97) it will do a lot of the hard work for you and find sites with good Google page rankings. Links still need to be submitted manually, though.

Another tool to use to find websites is WebFerret, which can be downloaded free from *www.webferret.com*. It finds all the sites that are linked to a particular site. You can use if for your own website but, more advantageously, you can look at sites you would like to link to, and see who they are linked to, giving you a massive "who's linked to who" map.

Go to each of the sites returned by the site-finder and make a list of those with a page rank of seven or above. Find email addresses and contact names for them and ask them to create a link to your site if they feel your content is relevant to their visitors. You could offer them something in exchange, e.g., access to content on your site for their visitors. If you and they are reputable, this process shouldn't present any problems.

When they have created a link, don't forget to email them to thank them for the link and to let them know you have created a link from your site to theirs and where they can find it.

If you prefer not to use this software, you can use Google to find the information; it will just take a little longer. For example, to find all the sites related or linked to the BBC website, type "related: www.bbc.co.uk" into the Google search bar and it will return a list of sites that are linked or that include information about the BBC. You could just as easily use "related: business coaches" as a search term.

When the links have been created on your website, use *www.webconfs.com/reciprocal-link-checker.php* to check they are working and *www.marketleap.com/publinkpop* to see how your linking strategy compares to that of other websites.

Internal Links – Don't Forget Them

Creating internal links on your website is also important as it helps to show relevancy and highlight keywords. Link keywords such as "marketing services" to your marketing services page, for example.

Remember, you have control over these links so be sure to use them and to choose your link words carefully: "click here" and "read more" links will not help your relevancy score. Choose links that are relevant and include at least one keyword from the target page. It is the words in the link – the anchor text - that Google uses to determine what the page being linked to is about, so it is essential the link includes a keyword.

If you can't avoid the "read more" approach, expand the link, e.g., "read more about our personal coaching services".

SEO-FRIENDLY DESIGN

It is important to make your website as easy as possible for the Googlebots and other search engine spiders to search. Here are some tips.

Sitemap

A sitemap is essentially a page on your website that lists the contents of the site and has internal links to every page. Internal links guide the Googlebots and other search engine spiders that visit your site. They provide an easy way to navigate your site and enable the bot to index your site efficiently. This is a sample of the site map from Apple's website, *www.apple.com/sitemap*

Apple.com Site Map

News & Events
Hot News
RSS Feeds
Product Presentations
eNews
Subscribe to eNews
eNews Schedule
Seminars & Events
User Groups

About Apple
Contacting Apple
Contacting Apple for Support and Service
Website Feedback
Job Opportunities
Investor Relations
Media Info
Web Badges
Environment
Accessibility
Responsible Supplier Management
Procurement
Legal Information
Privacy Information

Where to Buy
Where can I buy a Mac
Apple Store Online
Apple Store Online for Business
Apple Store Online for Education
Apple Store Online Country Selector
Apple Store Locations
Find a Reseller
Apple Financial Services

You could submit your sitemap to Google Webmaster tools, *www.google.com/webmaster/tools*. You will have to create an account and follow the steps to make some slight changes to your website, so that the Google bot will know that it is your site when it visits it. It can be time consuming, but it is worth doing.

Robot.txt

This is the first file search engine spiders look for when they visit your site and is included in the HTML code. By defining a few rules in this txt file, you can instruct the Googlebot not to crawl and index certain files on your site. For example, you might not want it to index the images directory on your site because it is irrelevant and shouldn't be displayed as a search result in Google.

It is also recommended that you use the robot.txt to direct the bot to your sitemap so it can index all the pages on your site.

Hidden Text

Having a website stuffed with keywords that are hidden or in white text will not help your cause. Search engine spiders got wise to this tactic a long time ago and are not fooled by it any more.

Duplicate Content

Don't duplicate content on your site to try to win favour with Google - it can be quite damaging to your rankings. And don't borrow content from elsewhere - Google checks for repetition and if it sees a lot of sites with similar content and cannot verify the source, it will downgrade them all.

Fresh Content

To maintain a good ranking for your site, you must add relevant fresh content on a regular basis. It keeps the bots coming back and gives them extra pages to index to gather more information about your site. Find the last time the Googlebot visited your page by clicking on the "cached" link in search results.

BBC - Homepage
bbc.co.uk offers a range of sites including news, sport, community, education, children's, and lifestyle sites, TV programme support, radio on demand, ...
www.bbc.co.uk/ - 45k - Cached - Similar pages

147

The time the page was last indexed or retrieved is displayed.

Flash™ and Javascript

Moving images can look great on your site, but they don't help with search engine optimisation. Developing a whole site using Flash™ isn't a complete no-no, but it will offer little or no content for the Googlebot to find and could have a detrimental effect on your rankings. If you want a Flash™ site, also have an HTML-based alternative site with real content that can be indexed by the bots and spiders.

Excessive use of Javascript on your site, for example, roll-over navigation bars, can be to blame for Google not indexing your site. Look at the cached version of your site and click on the "cached text" link to find out what content Google found when it visited your site.

W3C-compliant

There is a lot of debate about the best way to code HTML sites to increase search engine rankings. The World Wide Web Consortium (W3C) is an international body that sets web standards and guidelines - *www.w3.org*. One school of thought suggests that if you comply with their standards you will have a better chance of optimising your site. The jury is still out on the impact of compliance, but W3C standards provide a blueprint for an excellent and accessible website, so there is no harm in following their guidelines.

SITE DESIGN

Your site must be designed with the visitor in mind. If you do all the hard work to get ranked highly on Google, you should be confident that when visitors click through to your site they can find what need and like what they see. Here is a useful guide to help you establish whether your website gives visitors what they want.

Consistency

Your website must have a consistent look and feel so that, no matter where your visitor is on the site, they know they are still with the same company. There must be a common theme throughout the site and visitors must be able to find what they are looking for. Information should be easy to read, with keywords linked to relevant pages. Use plenty of white space, simple fonts and headlines to draw attention to specific content. Keep colours to a minimum and use accent colours for menu bars, etc.

Navigation

Make it easy for visitors to move around your site and to get back to where they started or to your home page. The menu bar should be in the same position on all pages. Avoid overly complex menus with roll-overs as they can be difficult to use. Make use of menus for search engine optimisation. For example, try using some keywords in the menu items. So, rather than the usual...

- About Us
- Our Services
- Our Products
- News
- Contact Us

We use...

- Marketing Experts
- Marketing Coaching
- Marketing Systems
- Free Marketing Articles
- Get Marketing Advice

It is helpful to direct visitors to the areas of the site that are most relevant to them. Some real estate and estate agencies do this very well: they ask the visitor if they want to buy, let or sell and take them to the appropriate pages. There is no reason why you shouldn't take a similar approach with your site by funnelling visitors to the pages most relevant to their needs.

Take Action

You want visitors to contact you as a result of visiting your website, so always prompt them to take action, or give them reasons to get in touch - download a guide, a no-obligation consultation, or product samples. Don't rely on them going to your contact page and calling you. Have your contact details on every page of the website, so they are easy for visitors to find.

Search

Provide a search box that enables visitors to search your site. If they are looking for something in particular and can't find it through the menus, they should be able to find it by searching the site.

Balance

Use a balanced combination of text, graphics and video. Don't rely on video, graphics or text alone. Too much text can turn off some visitors, so if you are explaining a concept, consider using an image or video to illustrate it. The key is not to have too much of one thing and to have a website that is accessible and easy to use.

Throughout this book we recommended using specialists to help you with your marketing - SEO is no different. It is a highly specialised field and, while this chapter gives you the basics, it is always worth talking to an expert internet marketer if you really want to optimise your rankings in Google and other search engines.

SEO CHECKLIST

This checklist will help to ensure you include all the elements we have covered as part of your SEO strategy. Or you could use it to guide discussions with your SEO specialist.

- ☐ **Site map** – Develop a site map of all the content you want to include on your website and how pages link.

- ☐ **Keyword and key phrases** – Develop the keywords and key phrases you want to use; research them to find out how effective they will be, using a tool such as Keyword tracker.

- ☐ **Developing content** – Plan each page of content on your website with individual keywords that are related to that page and unique title and description meta tags.

- ☐ **Links** – Research sites you benefit from linking to and from. Include these links on your site and ensure you have links to your site from other relevant high-ranking sites. Don't forget that internal links on your site are important - ensure your keywords are linked to content on your site.

- ☐ **Web design** – Create a site that is clear about its purpose, represents your company brand and values effectively, is easy to navigate and encourages the visitor to find out more. Use search engine-friendly code that points to your site map and enables spiders to index the content effectively.

BLOGS

Blogs seem to be the greatest new way to get yourself noticed on the internet, but how many of us really know how they work or what they can do for our business?

Basically, a blog, or weblog, is simply an online journal, diary or commentary where a person or business posts regular thoughts, articles and ideas they want to share with the world. In some instances, they invite readers to comment on what they have written. Increasingly, however, the blog is becoming more than an insight into an individual's life – blogs are being used by businesses around the world to promote their expertise.

How A Blog Can Help Your Business

It provides a platform to include all sorts of information, thoughts and ideas that you may not want to include on your main site. You could include articles or small stories about business experiences related to your products and services, as well as talking about innovations or changes in legislation within your industry.

If you are thinking of publishing a blog, you must keep the content current and contribute regularly. We once visited a blog where the most recent posting was more than a year old. The point of a blog is that it is current and carries relevant information. If you are already maxed out with other marketing activities, ask yourself if you have the time and resources to do a blog justice before you commit to it. You will have to update it at least every week and include new articles at least every two. Bots and search engine spiders love blogs as they provide consistently fresh content, so be sure you can give it to them.

According to Claire Rikes, of the Business Blog Angel (*www.businessblogangel.com*), there are eight immediate benefits from creating a business blog:

1. A blog is great for pulling in traffic on specific topics you are writing about. Because you update your blog on a regular basis, the search engine spiders will begin to rank your site and they like blogs as they generally contain good, relevant information.

2. A blog provides a personal face and brand platform. For example, the blog could be written by the technical team and could highlight their expertise and provide ideas and tips.

3. A blog positions you as an expert – this is one of the great things about blogs. You can talk about your industry, innovations, thoughts and ideas. It doesn't always have to be product-related and highlights your knowledge.

4. A blog creates a rapport and builds trust – if your content is full of rich and interesting thoughts and comments about your industry, people are likely to visit your blog regularly to find out what you are saying and you begin to build trust with potential clients.

5. A blog builds a network or community around you. By inviting comments and regularly commenting back, you can build a

community. If you include an RSS news feed on your site, subscribers will be notified when you post new content. This is a great way of getting potential clients to visit your blog regularly and for you to collect names and email addresses.

6. Blogs provide lots of opportunities to capture information about your target market. You can run polls, include links to your information or run competitions.

7. Blogs are perfect for podcasting– run your own radio show, set times when you will talk about a particular subject and broadcast to the world.

8. Blogs allow you to be more creative with audio and video – you can include videos of presentations, or recordings of your seminars.

Even Boeing has a blog. Randy, a technical expert who has been with the company for over 25 years, posts new information about the aerospace industry, their new planes and engineering products. Take a look at *http://boeingblogs.com/randy*

How Do I Set Up A Blog?

Lots of sites specialise in blogs. They are usually free or may charge a small monthly fee, depending on how much you want to brand and customise your blog. They will even host the blog for you - all you have to do is set up an account, use one of their templates to design your blog and then add your content. The major blogging sites are:

- *www.typepad.com* – business-focused
- *www.wordpress.com* – business-focused
- *www.blogger.com* – free and more for personal use, but can work for a business

If you don't want to set up your own blog but would still like to have one, there are online consultants who will do it for you very cost effectively:

- *www.businessblogangel.com*
- *www.stevewatsononline.com*
- *http://michaelmartine.com/blog-consulting* - includes a free e-book with a 12-step process for starting your business blog

Remember, a blog can be a highly effective way of promoting your expertise and knowledge and of bringing new clients to you door. However, you must have the time to keep it up to date with relevant content and be committed to posting articles and information on a regular basis.

PAY-PER-CLICK ADVERTISING – DON'T BURN YOUR CASH

Pay-per-click (PPC) advertising through search engines such as Google and MSN can be an effective way of generating instant traffic for your site. You can set up your adverts within a day or so and can see instantly how well they work and what your conversion rates are from click-through to purchase or enquiry through tools like Google Analytics. SEO work is more involved and takes much longer to produce results.

However, PPC can be costly and if you don't fully understand how the system works you can end up spending a lot of cash for very little return. If you want to proceed, you must either spend a long time learning how to write and target adverts, how to track your competitors and researching keywords. Or you could employ a professional who can set up your Google or MSN PPC accounts for you, create the adverts and work on getting good conversion rates.

If you favour the first route, probably the best investment you can make is to buy The Definitive Guide to AdWords by Perry Marshall. It will give you all the information you need, from setting up your account and creating adverts to bidding competitively for keywords and controlling your budget. The guide costs around £50 ($100) and contains a great deal of useful information that could save you wasting thousands on Google adverts. You can buy the guide at *www.perrymarshall.com*.

Google provides a lot of information about how its service works at *https://adwords.google.com*. The site includes tutorials and information to help you set up your Adword campaign.

A useful free e-book by Arron Matthew Wall, which gives a good overview of PPC and some great tips on how to create ad campaigns and find keywords that will work for you, can be downloaded from *www.seobook.com/overture-adwords.pdf.*

Be aware that it will take time to learn the intricacies of Google Adwords. If you don't have the time or inclination, hire the services of someone who does. Always check their credentials and ask to talk to some of their clients to find out what results they are getting for other companies. You need to be confident they know what they are doing and that you won't be wasting your cash on consultancy fees and adverts that don't work.

These companies could help:

- *www.simplifyinternetmarketing.co.uk*
- *www.simplifytheinternet.com*
- *www.bruceclay.com* or *www.bruceclay.co.uk*

We are not Google PPC experts, but here are some basic tips and guidance that you might find useful.

What Is Pay-Per-Click?
Pay-per-click adverts do exactly what they say they will. By applying a chosen keyword or phrase, your advert will be displayed on your chosen site, e.g. Google or MSN. If your advert is sufficiently appealing to the person who has keyed in a particular search term, they will click on your advert and go through to your site. For that, you will be charged a fee - you have paid for a click. There is no saying what that person will do once they get to your site, whether they will convert to buying some products or request further information or even leave if they don't find what they are looking for.

How Much Does It Cost?
The fee charged per click depends on a number of variables, such as the time of day you want your adverts to appear and the number of other advertisers who also want to appear for that keyword, i.e., how competitive the search term is. The more competitive the keyword, the more you will have to pay for your advert to appear near the top of the PPC adverts.

To find out how much your competitors are paying, you could use the Spyfu tool (*www.spyfu.com*). It tells you which keywords your competitors are buying and which ones they optimise their sites for. Once you understand the competition, you can beat them at their own game and/or exploit their weaknesses.

The key to successful pay-per-click campaigns is choosing the right keywords. As with search engine optimisation, the right keywords will bring the right clients through to your website. You should spend time working out what your main keywords are, how competitive they are and whether they will attract your target audience.

For example, if we were running a Google PPC campaign, the keyword "marketing" would be far too broad for us. If we wanted to appear on the first page of Google above our "marketing" competitors, we would have to pay a high price per click. The people who came through to our site would have a general interest in marketing but not in business-to-business marketing; we probably wouldn't covert many of them; and we would have a large bill.

You can see that choosing the right keywords or phrases for your PPC campaign is absolutely vital and it can take time and effort to find keywords that are relevant to your business but not hugely competitive. As with SEO, start by using a tool such as Keyword Tracker (*www.keywordtracker.com*) to find your keywords. Then if you want to do more research, use tools such as Adword Accelerator (*www.adwordaccelerator.com*) or Adword Analyzer (*www.adwordanalyzer.com*). They take your main keywords and suggest other related keywords to consider. Then they take each related keyword and drill down further into it, finding even more specific keyword variations worth targeting that your competitors aren't using.

The Google Keyword Suggestion Tool is free - *https://adwords.google.com/select/KeywordToolExternal*. It estimates search volume, trends and advertising competition. You can enter a keyword to analyse or it can extract relevant keywords from a given page. You could use it in conjunction with the Google Traffic Estimator (*https://adwords.google.co.uk/select/TrafficEstimatorSandbox*), which estimates the price of ranking number one on Adwords for 85% of the time and the traffic you can expect from Google Adwords for a given bid.

When you have set up your keywords and created your adverts, set a limit for your daily spend. Once your budget has been used up, your advert will stop appearing. So, if you have a budget of £10 ($20) per day and you are bidding for highly competitive keywords at £2 ($4) per click, your advert won't appear for long. However, if you are savvy and choose less competitive keywords that are still relevant to your target audience, your budget will last much longer.

Also, statistics show that lower positions on Google yield better click-through rates. If you are on a tight budget, it is better to occupy position eight for the whole day on a tightly targeted keyword, than position two on a more general keyword for only 25% of the time.

Your PPC Advert

The content of your advert will determine whether it is clicked on by prospective clients – and as you can see you have only a few words to get your message across. These results below are for an "industrial water pumps" search. There are quite a few PPC adverts on the right-hand side:

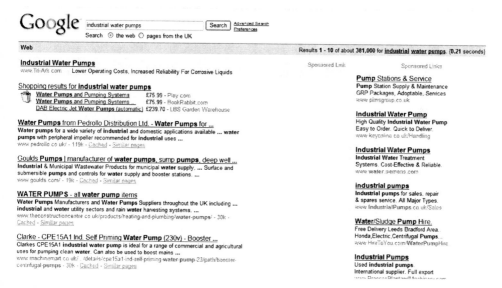

The key to creating a good advert is to include the keyword or phrase being searched for in the title - "industrial water pumps". Then you must include compelling copy that will prompt a visit to your site. In the example above, the second advert down, seems to match what the individual was looking for: ordering is easy and delivery is prompt. It seems reasonable to expect a click-through.

However the fifth advert down, isn't relevant to the search term, it is related in some way as it is, "water/sludge pump hire" and although it talks about free delivery, it is in the Leeds/Bradford area of the UK. If the person running the search was based in London, or anywhere else in the world, they wouldn't click on the advert.

It is absolutely essential that your advert works for you. You could offer a free guide or tips based on the search term; you must include words that prompt action and get qualified prospects to visit your site. To find out more about this subject, see the e-book *'How to Write Successful PPC Ads' - www.writeppcads.com.*

Your Landing Page

If you or your PPC consultant has gone to all the hard work of finding the right keywords, bidding at the right price and developing a killer advert, then the last thing you want to do is to take the prospective client to you home page. You must create a specific landing page which relates to the keyword and the advert the visitor has clicked on and is highly relevant to what they are looking for and convinces the visitor to stay.

Here are some tips on what you can to do to improve your landing pages:

- **You must capture attention immediately**. When the visitor arrives on your landing page you have only seconds to persuade them to stay, they need to see immediately what's in it for them. The information on the top half of your page matters more than any other content - it is what the visitor sees when they click through from your advert. They shouldn't be expected scroll down to find the information they are looking for.

- **Repeat the keyword or phrase** they searched for in your headline and tell them how you can help them. Your headline must stand out and make them take action. If you offered a free guide or "white paper", use a picture of it with download instructions and a killer headline that makes them want to download it straight away. Pay particular attention to the first few lines of copy after the headline and be sure to highlight the benefits of your product or guide; remind them why they need to take action.

- **Only sell what they are looking for.** To secure good conversion rates from your adverts, only give the visitor the information they are looking for. Don't include background on the company or information about other products and services - keep the page focused on what you promised in the advert. If possible, aim for a plain landing page without lots of navigation to tempt the visitor away - if they go digging around your site, you won't convert them. Consider including footer navigation in a text format or a link to your home page once they have taken up your offer.

- **Be brief but concise.** Most visitors don't actually read landing pages, they just scan them. A strong headline with the benefits bullet-pointed and keywords or phrases in bold will grab their attention. A short audio clip or video will engage the visitor and make them want to listen to or watch what you have to say.

- **Gather only relevant information.** If you want information from a potential client in return for a guide or "white paper", only ask for what you really need. Being asked for lots of information can put people off. As a minimum, ask for their name, company and email address - you can contact them later to find out more.

- **Follow-up or conversion page.** Don't forget to say thank you. After the person has provided their information, take them to a thank you page to let them know what will happen next and include a link to your website's home page or blog.

Tracking and Testing

You need to know if your adverts work and are converting clicks into clients, or are at least delivering qualified enquiries, and the real cost per click. Google allows you to test multiple adverts at any given time, so you can try out different adverts for certain keywords or phrases. This enables you to see which adverts have the best click-through rates and which ones don't work.

If you have an advert that is creating a good click-through rate, copy it and send visitors to a different landing page from the duplicate and you will find out which page converts more visitors. Google offers a landing page testing software program called Google Website Optimiser (*www.google.com/websiteoptimizer*) which tells you which of your landing pages is likely to work better and tests them for you in real time.

To find out how your adverts are working and where your visitors are coming from, use Google Analytics (*www.google.com/analytics*). This tool will produce statistics on your campaigns, helping you to write better ads, strengthen your marketing initiatives and create higher-converting websites.

Keep testing until you find relevant keywords that make people click on your killer advert and convert through an amazing landing page. Remember, if this isn't a core skill for you and you don't want to spend time learning it, work with a professional who will do all this for you and keep testing until they create cost-effective Google PPC campaigns that deliver qualified prospects who convert into leads or purchase your products and services.

BANNER ADVERTISING

Banner adverts on websites visited by your target audience are another way of driving traffic to your website. Banner advertising is similar to display advertising in print - select websites your prospective client is likely to visit and place a strong advert with a call to action in a prominent position. Here is an example of a banner advert for Citrix on Computing magazine's website:

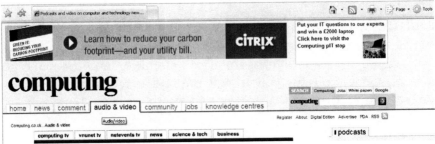

What Makes A Good Banner Advert?

It is most important to make your banner adverts visually appealing and to place them on web pages visited by your target audience with relevant content.

Here are just a few tips to consider when designing a banner advert:

- **Have a call to action or offer.** Rather than just advertise your website - it could be a guide, seminar or audit, as long as it is something that is of interest to your potential client. Remember, there has to be something in it for them to click through.

- **Link to a landing page.** As with PPC advertising, once a prospect clicks on your advert you must take them through to a persuasive landing page that gets them to download the guide. The guidelines we mentioned in the previous section about creating great landing pages apply.

- **Position is important.** Find out the best positions on a page and which achieve the best click-through rates from the advertising salesperson. Consider booking a specific page that is related to your product or service, rather than the home page. Often the best positions are the banner adverts at the top of the page, but this isn't necessarily the case, so always ask.

- **Use simple messages.** State what the offer is and how to act on it. If possible, use a graphic such as picture of the guide or "white paper" to show them what they will get by clicking through.

- **Use animated adverts.** Most websites offer animated adverts where you have two or three frames to get your message across. You can build up your message from "are you interested in...?" through to "then you need this" and "click here to download".

How Much Do Banner Adverts Cost?

Different websites have different ways of charging for banner adverts. In the main, they will quote a CPM (cost per mille or thousand), a media term describing the cost of 1,000 impressions. Expect to pay from £5 to £100 per 1,000 impressions on a popular site. A site with high traffic will usually charge a lot more than a less popular site.

Advertising is usually sold in packages of 50,000 to 200,000 impressions, so if your CPM is £15 and the site records 50,000 impressions in a month, you will pay £750 per month for your advert.

However, if you find a smaller niche website that doesn't get a huge volume of traffic but is relevant to your products and services, the cost may be much lower. Don't be put off by fewer page impressions - it is very likely that most of the visitors to the site will be in your target market, so, although there are fewer of them, they are likely to be interested in your offer.

Without talking to advertising executives at each website, it is difficult to estimate a monthly advertising cost. Many do not provide CPM rates for specific pages and concentrate instead on the CPM of the home page. There is always room for negotiation and if the website is small and niche, you might get a good rate because visitor numbers are lower.

9. Strategies For Keeping The Clients You Have

"When you stop talking, you've lost your customer. When you turn your back, you've lost her."
ESTEE LAUDER

We recently received this email from one of our suppliers; it is real life example of what a large company allowed one of their new members of staff to send out to existing clients. We have re-typed it, including all the errors but have removed the name of the organisation to save the blushes of the company involved. But this is how it went...

Subject: Account Manager – New Point of Contact

Hi

I have tried to contact you but have been unsuccessful. I just wanted to introduce myself, you probably dealt with Sarah in regarding to any of our services you required however she no longer works for the company. I am your new account manager and main point of contact her at Acme Company and will look after you best I can. If you can let me know your direct contact details and advice me if you have anything you need me to work on, also if you could advice me of any other people on the company that may require our services so I can introduce me to them I would be very grateful.

If you don't need our service then let me know and I won't get in touch with you again.

Kind regards

We don't buy a great deal from them, but who knows how many people who dealt with Sarah on a regular basis saw this email? The spelling errors and lack of thought that went into it create a bad impression. And, to add insult to injury, it ends with the assertion that "I only want to talk to you if you are interested in our services" - not the best way to make friends and influence people!

Keeping existing clients is just as important as finding new ones - you must make every effort to keep in touch with them and make them aware of new products and services. If you don't, your competitors will!

"WE MUST KEEP IN TOUCH..."

How often have you said to a friend or colleague that you must keep in touch and really meant it, but failed to do so? Time seems to fly by and, before you realise it, months and then years go by and you lose touch. Other things get in the way - work, relationships and family matters - and while you wonder what has happened to them, you never seem to have the time to send an email or pick up the phone. The same may apply to them: they may have lost your details or have moved on to new job opportunities.

Then one day you look them up on Friends Reunited or Linked In and find they have been leading a parallel life or are employed by a company you would like to work for. If only you had kept in touch... or contacted them sooner...

New Clients Vs Loyal Clients

Is the same true for your clients? Have you been so busy chasing new business that you have forgotten the rich seam of revenue in existing clients? If only you had taken the time to maintain contact with them and keep them abreast of what was happening, you could open up new revenue streams.

Keeping In Contact

There are several reasons to keep in touch with existing and lapsed clients, including:

- **You may have new or additional services or products** that would be of interest to them. Companies often find clients have gone to a competitor because they "didn't realise you could make super widgets as well as basic sprockets". Keep your clients updated with news and information on a regular basis.

- **Your clients can be a great source of referrals.** If you have done a great job for a client, ask if any of their clients or colleagues could be referred to you. It works and it ensures that you retain a link with a client even if the project has finished.

- **Loyalty brings rewards.** Keeping in touch, providing useful help and information such as guides or articles, keeps your brand in their mind, ensuring they don't forget about you. A regular email or newsletter is a simple way of contacting them.

- **Make that call.** Call lapsed clients to find out how they are getting on or to let them know you have a new product or service that may interest them. Just because they haven't contacted you, that is no reason not to give them a call once a quarter.

- **Follow the leader.** If your contact leaves the company you supply, find out where their new job is. Thank them for their business to date and let them know you will be in touch for a chat when they have had a chance to settle in. Also, find out who is taking over their role and arrange to meet them.

- **Word of mouth.** By providing a great service and keeping in touch with existing and lapsed clients, you re-enforce the fact that you are a great organisation to work with. Word of mouth is one of the most under-used marketing tools. If you are being talked about in a positive way, prospective clients will get to hear about it.

- **Great news.** If you see articles relating to your client's industry or about them, send them a copy of the editorial or a link to the website. Let them know you were thinking about them and that their news is important to you.

Knowing Your Clients

As with friends, keeping track of clients is highly important when you are running a successful business. The company you supplied with 100 widgets, two years ago may have grown into a large company ordering 1,000 widgets from your closest competitor.

Your clients are the lifeblood of your company; without them you wouldn't survive. Don't let them drift away. Keep them close to you and stay in touch, even if it is only through a Christmas card or twice-yearly newsletter. Build existing clients into your marketing plans and devote time to keeping them loyal and thinking about you in a positive way, even if you aren't working with them any more. Make the effort - you may be surprised at the rewards it can bring.

MARKETING ACTIVITIES FOR EXISTING AND LAPSED CLIENTS

Here are some marketing activities that focus on keeping your clients and those you haven't been in touch with for some time.

Client Forum

Find clients who have similar businesses and host a regular forum or round-table event where they can get together to discuss industry issues and best practice. Run the forum or club every couple of months and invite 10 to 20 of your best clients to discuss a particular subject. Let them know they have been selected to join this elite forum or club because of the knowledge and experience they can contribute. The forum will also give them an opportunity to network with peers and to find out how other companies have overcome issues and challenges. You also win because you get your clients talking about issues and problems you might not have been aware of and that you can help them with.

Newsletter or E-bulletin

We only recommend sending newsletters to people who know you or have specifically requested this type of information via a subscription box on your website. How often you produce a newsletter and the format it takes are up to you. Remember, you will have to find the time to write the articles and, if you decide to have a physical newsletter (rather than an e-bulletin that includes links to articles on your web page) fund printing and postage costs.

Articles in your newsletter must be related to your industry or about new products or services you are launching. Keep births, deaths, marriages, company nights out, promotions, etc, out of your newsletter. The most successful newsletters include useful articles that are about your area of expertise. They should be informative and not be full of blatant promotions. We regularly send out an e-bulletin that contains links to useful marketing articles on our website (*www.brightermarketing.com*), and it is a great tool for us to keep in touch with our referral partners, clients, prospects and people who have subscribed to our newsletter.

Hospitality

Making your clients feel valued is important and arranging special events where they get an opportunity to meet you and your other clients can be a good way of maintaining their loyalty. There are hundreds of ways you can do this: bowling nights, golf days, racing days, or even just an open day at your offices. Whatever you do, if you choose a hospitality event that is suited to your target audience, they will find some value in attending.

For example, if you know that 90% of your clients play golf, organise an inter-company golf tournament. Find the events that strike a chord with your clients and get them involved. While they are at the event, encourage them to interact with you and your team and provide opportunities for them to talk to your other clients.

You could develop a series of private dinners and lunch meetings for your clients. Hire a private dining room in a good restaurant, invite five of your clients, and ask each of them to bring along a colleague from another company. You get to talk to your existing clients and hopefully meet some new ones, all in a relaxed setting.

10. Database – Your Most Valuable Marketing Tool

"Now that we have all this useful information, it would be nice to do something with it."
UNIX PROGRAMMERS MANUAL

The cornerstone of your marketing is keeping track of your prospects and clients and recording relevant information about them that will help your marketing to become more and more effective. Your database, contact management system (CMS) or customer relationship management (CRM) software is one of the most under-used marketing tools at your disposal. Imagine losing all your client data - where would your business be?

As your organisation moves towards becoming a marketing-orientated organisation, having a database to manage clients and prospects will play an important role. It will enable you to be more aware of the mix and diversity of your client base, to know who has bought what and when, and to keep track of marketing campaigns, etc.

However, before you rush out and invest in new software or start to overhaul your current system, stop and think about what you want your database to do. Create a document that outlines the type of information you want to record and how the database will be used. Remember, any software you use is just an enabler: you need to know how you are going to use it first.

The diagram overleaf outlines the key project milestones to consider when developing a new database system. For some readers the approach may be too detailed, but it gives you an idea of the kind of thought you should put into developing your database

Database Milestones

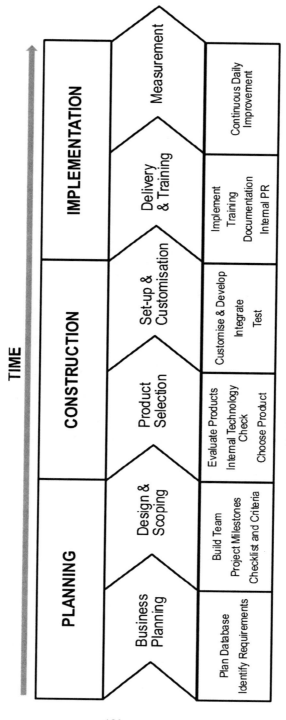

TIME

PLANNING	CONSTRUCTION	IMPLEMENTATION

Business Planning
Plan Database
Identify Requirements

Design & Scoping
Build Team
Project Milestones
Checklist and Criteria

Product Selection
Evaluate Products
Internal Technology Check
Choose Product

Set-up & Customisation
Customise & Develop
Integrate
Test

Delivery & Training
Implement
Training
Documentation
Internal PR

Measurement
Continuous Daily Improvement

PLANNING YOUR DATABASE – A SAMPLE DOCUMENT

The following section includes information you can use to develop your database document, to ensure that whether you update an existing database or invest in new technology, you have scoped out what you want and why.

This is a sample document you can use as the basis for your planning.

Use

The database system should give employees appropriate access to information that enables them to operate effectively within their role. This includes sales information, marketing campaign information, progress of prospects and current information about clients. Moreover, it should provide the reports necessary to give senior management an overview of prospects and clients, their status, what they have purchased and their revenue to date.

The accuracy and quality of the data contained within the database will be key to its use. Contacts must be kept up to date. The database should be used to keep accurate records of sales progress so that the senior management team can produce realistic sales forecasts and gain relevant information about key opportunities and client accounts.

Before a CRM solution is sourced, purchased and implemented, the following functionality and integration aspects should be considered.

Customisation & User-Defined Fields

The ability to customise the database is essential. The development of extra user-defined fields to record important information will help with maintaining accurate records as the company grows. This includes adding fields that may not be included as part of the standard set-up, e.g. products purchased, marketing responded to. This will enable searches to be performed that build reports on the status of certain accounts, e.g. all clients who have bought green widgets.

Usability

The solution must be easy to use and should not significantly increase the workload of users. Effective training should be included as part of the roll-out to ensure the system can be used properly and efficiently. Users must always enter accurate information and complete all the necessary details, enabling future searches for information to return accurate results and to ensure the correct data is provided for reports.

Library

It is important that the quality of information sent electronically to clients and prospects is consistent, so a library of marketing literature, such as PDF files, should be made available centrally. This will ensure that clients are sent the most appropriate information via email.

Templates

Templates for all documentation sent to contacts should be created and held centrally. This will ensure all correspondence materials are consistent and reflect company branding at all times and enable the creation of standard letters, etc.

Calendar

This ensures effective forward planning of sales resource time.

Email Integration

Communication via email is now an essential part of business life. The database should integrate with Outlook to both send and receive email so that an accurate record of email activity can be kept.

General Functionality

Functionality, i.e. the type of information the database needs to hold, is outlined below. It is important to detail the critical data to be held as this will have an impact on how the system is used.

There should be an overview of each prospect/client, their status and comprehensive notes on meetings, etc. This is essential when building a client-focused organisation. The following data would be vital to our company:

- **Organisation details** – company name, address, web, switchboard etc.

- **Contact details** for each relevant individual within the organisation, site address, DDI numbers, mobiles and job title, e.g. Managing Director, Finance Director.

- **Opportunities** – Prospects, i.e. sales opportunities, can be clearly identified, detailing the probability of closing business and the value.

- **Documents** – Electronic copies of all documents associated with an account, such as letters and proposals, can be attached to the contact and are available to view.

- **Calls** – Accurate records of all calls made to individual contacts and outcomes can be noted and viewed.

- **Email** – Integration with Outlook possible so that emails can be recorded for individual contacts.

- **Follow-up** – Reminders to call regarding follow-up to direct mail or a sales meeting can be placed on individual contacts. This should prompt a message to call when an individual logs on to the database.

- **Record of products and services sold**– Accurate information on the product and services sold to clients can be recorded.

- **Notes** – Relevant account information that does not relate to phone calls and other communications can be recorded.

- **Status** – Pre-defined fields are available to record active, inactive, etc, clients.

- **Calendar** – Shows where the company sales team is on a daily basis.

Marketing Functionality

The ability to use the database to accurately record and track leads is important. This should include:

- **Marketing literature library** – a library of marketing information in PDF form that can be searched and attached to emails sent to clients and prospects.

- **Templates** – a range of branded templates for documents and emails should be available to ensure all communication from the company is co-ordinated and promotes the brand at all times.

- **Source** – the sources of leads should be recorded in pre-defined fields, e.g. seminar, networking, referral, etc.
- **Telemarketing** – there should be a facility to record calls to prospects and their key responses, as well as conversations via telemarketing.
- **Conversion** – ability to show conversion from a lead to a client via pre-defined fields - an important measurement.

Reporting

Reports produced from the database will provide vital management and sales information. The ability to build both standard and bespoke reports should be considered. Below is the type of information that should be easily retrievable as long as appropriate user-defined fields are set up and the data entered accurately.

Marketing

A range of reports that will assist with targeted marketing for direct mail campaigns. Suggestions include:

- Build data for direct mail campaigns based on postcode, type of company, type of product interest.
- Outline response to direct mail campaigns and flag for telephone follow-up.
- Show ROI on campaigns through conversion rates.

Sales

A wide range of sales reports can be built within a CRM system to give senior management pertinent information on which to base business decisions. Here are some examples of the types of reports that could be built on a weekly/monthly basis:

- Forecasts and pipeline information for individual sales people.
- Trends, types of products and services purchased and frequency.
- Conversion rates from lead to sale.
- Calendar reports – who is doing what and when.
- Overview of notes on key accounts.

CRM Team

Roles and responsibilities for those involved in the implementation of the database should be defined from the outset. This will ensure each person understands their objectives and how they will work with other team members to achieve successful implementation. Some or all of the following will be required:

- **Overall project manager** – keeps the project on schedule and ensures all aspects of the project are taken into consideration. They should positively promote the use of the solution to users internally before implementation.

- **Technical manager** – a key person responsible for the implementation of the system, ensures the CRM solution works in your environment.

- **Consultant** – Required for customisation of the solution and to work with the Technical Manager and Project Manager to ensure successful set-up and implementation of the solution. It is likely their knowledge will be product specific; expert knowledge can be essential when implementing a database for the first time.

Technical Considerations

It is important to consider the existing technical environment in your company before purchasing a solution as it will have an impact on the implementation and timescales. Time should be taken to understand the following:

- What type of PCs or workstations are in use? What is their operating system, e.g. Windows Vista or XP, and is it supported by the CRM solution? Is this consistent across the company?

- Are any extra development tools required to implement the solution? What servers are in place? Will they support the solution?

- How will the solution integrate with existing systems, e.g., Sage or Quick Books?

- Are any specific technical skills required to implement the solution and for ongoing support?

Data Migration

It is important that current client and prospect data is migrated to the new database and that the quality of this data is validated for use in the new database. If information is out of date or of poor quality, serious consideration should be given to its use in the new solution.

If you are unable to export the data from the current system, you must consider the cost of entering the data. This could be time-consuming and have an impact on the timescales for implementation.

Managing Expectations

It is vital that the implementation of the database is managed positively within your company. Employees should be kept abreast of significant milestones and the benefits to both them and the company explained via briefing sessions. They must feel comfortable with the changes and understand why the solution is being used. Also, full training will be required to ensure that all employees who will use the new system understand its benefits and how to use it effectively. This includes guidelines for inputting data to ensure information in the database remains accurate and up-to-date.

Cost

The cost of buying in a database solution should also be considered; it involves more than purchasing a product. The following costs should be taken into account:

- **Purchase of solution** – including licences for users, server and ongoing annual renewal licences.
- **Purchase of additional software** – may include database software or, e.g. updating all users to the same version of Windows.
- **Support** – level of support required for both the set-up and implementation phase and ongoing support?

- **Consultancy** – is a consultant with specific product knowledge required to assist with the technical implementation, the set-up and customisation?
- **Training** – what costs will be associated with providing training for employees using the solution?
- **Data Input** – what will be the cost of inputting initial data accurately?

Choosing A Solution

Choosing a solution should be a considered process. It is crucial that the database meets your requirements. You should base your decision on the information in this section, from pricing to technical suitability.

Suggested software products:

- Act!
- Sales Logix
- Maximizer
- Goldmine
- Salesforce.com

Don't rush into buying a database solution. Don't see the suppliers until you know what you want or you could end up buying technology that has to be shoe horned into your business model. You are in control so you should know what questions to ask potential suppliers to establish whether their solution meets your needs. Consider talking to some of their existing customers to find out how they use the solution and if it works for them.

11. Focus & Planning – Be Prepared

"In preparing for battle I have always found that plans are useless, but planning is indispensable."
DWIGHT D. EISENHOWER

This book wouldn't be complete without a chapter on marketing planning. If your marketing is to succeed, you need to know what to do, when to do it and how much it costs. *Chapter 2* talks about needing to know where your company is heading and developing marketing objectives. However, now that you have identified all the marketing tools at your disposal, you need to take it one step further and develop a plan to keep you focused on your marketing.

The type of plan you develop will depend on what you need. Some companies want a marketing plan they can use to secure a marketing budget from the board of directors. Other companies just want a spreadsheet that shows the timing of a marketing activity and the cost involved.

Whatever approach you take, you must commit time to plan your marketing and work out the budget you need to achieve your goals.

We have included a simple marketing plan template to use if you want to be more specific about your marketing approach. In addition, we have provided some sample spreadsheets to support your marketing plan or you could use one of your own if you just want to develop a marketing schedule.

SAMPLE MARKETING PLAN TEMPLATE

These are the headings we suggest for your marketing plan. You may not need them all, so choose the ones you want for your organisation.

Key Actions or Executive Summary

When you have completed the other sections, come back to this first section and list the key marketing actions you are going to take over the next 12 months. This is like an executive summary and will give anyone reading the plan a real feeling of what you want to achieve and summarise your key points.

Our Vision

Detail the company's overall vision and be specific about the goals you want to achieve.

How Will Marketing Help Us Achieve Our Vision?

In this section, detail your marketing objectives and explain how your marketing approach will help you achieve your company vision.

The Opportunity

If you have identified a significant market opportunity through your marketing gap analysis that you want to take advantage of, mention it here. Outline what the opportunity is and include any market research you have done to back up your recommendations.

The Competition – Who Do We Need To Beat?

You could include an analysis of the competition, what they are doing and where you feel you have an advantage over them or need to improve the perception of your products and services.

Who Are We?

This section deals with your brand – is there a need for changes to your logo or the way your brand is perceived? Or is it OK as it is?

What Are We Selling?

In this section, be very precise about your product and service range and detail exactly what you will be selling over the next year. Also include information on what you are really selling - all the emotive information we covered in *Chapter 3* that will drive clients to buy from you.

Who Are We Selling To?

Be clear about who you are targeting and list your target criteria according to the type of company and the decision-makers you are looking for. If the information is available, include figures on the number of decision-makers you want to target over the next 12 months, where the data will come from and any costs involved.

Marketing Activities

This section should include all the marketing activities you will undertake, why you are doing them, the costs and roles and responsibilities. Create a table for each one using the headings below:

ACTIVITY	WHY	BUDGET	ROLES & RESP

How Will We Work With Sales?

Outline how any leads produced as a result of marketing activities will be followed up by the sales team to generate appointments or sales.

How Will The Marketing Plan Be Implemented?

Describe how you will implement the plan with your current resources and state whether you will need more support or new team members with particular skills to help you achieve your marketing objectives.

How Will We Measure Success?

Include information on the type of results you hope to achieve through marketing, so that you can gauge how successful your marketing has been. *Chapter 14* provides some information on how to measure your marketing - you could include some of these measurements in this section.

SAMPLE MARKETING PLANNING SPREADSHEETS

We have developed three types of spreadsheets for marketing planning: a six-month overview, weekly and daily planning sheets. These can be found on the following pages.

Marketing Overview: activity, task, responsibility, cost

This spreadsheet enables you to list the basis tasks for each of the marketing activities you will undertake, the cost and who is responsible for them. It gives a monthly total as well as a running six-month total. You can, if wish, extend this to 12 months to give an annual budget and overview of your activities and spend.

ACTIVITY	RESPONSIBILITY	JAN	FEB	MAR	APR	MAY	JUN	
								£2,609
DIRECT MAIL								
Design	Design Co.	£1,500						
Copy	Sarah Jones							
Printing	Printers	£750						
Fulfilment	XYZ Distribution	£359						
ACTIVITY 2								
ACTIVITY 3								
ACTIVITY 4								
COST		£2,609	£0	£0	£0	£0	£0	

Weekly Planner

This weekly planner enables you to look at each of your marketing activities in more detail and to see what is happening each month, and what should be completed when on a week-by-week basis. You could use different coloured blocks to identify responsibility rather than standard black ones.

		ACTIVITY 1	Subtask 1	Subtask 2	Subtask 3	Subtask 4	Completion	ACTIVITY 2				ACTIVITY 3			
MONTH 4	WK4														
	WK3														
	WK2														
	WK1														
MONTH 3	WK4														
	WK3														
	WK2														
	WK1														
MONTH 2	WK4														
	WK3						■								
	WK2					■									
	WK1					■									
MONTH 1	WK4					■									
	WK3			■	■										
	WK2			■											
	WK1		■												

Daily Planner

This daily planner takes the weekly planner into more detail and you could use it for projects that demand a greater level of detail. As with the weekly planner, you could assign different coloured blocks to identify responsibility for each task.

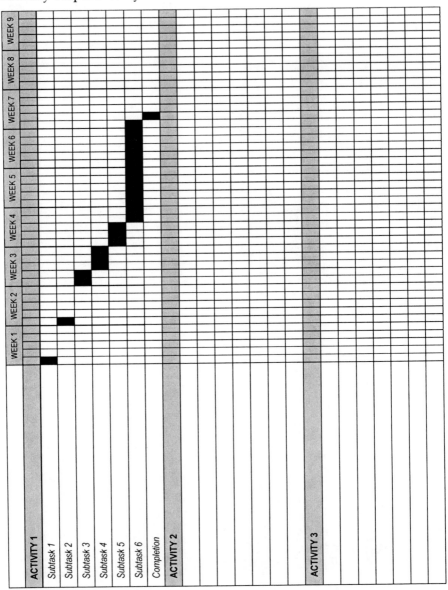

12. Choosing an Agency or Freelancer

*"If we are together nothing is impossible.
If we are divided all will fail."*
WINSTON CHURCHILL

Throughout this book we provide guidance on how you can get the most out of your marketing, but there will be times when you need expert help - with web design, direct mail creativity or search engine optimisation. You use accountants, solicitors and other professionals because they have expert knowledge and the same should apply to your marketing: if you need assistance, take the time to find a partner who can help you.

There are many types of agencies and freelancers specialising in areas ranging from graphic design and PR to research. Some offer a selection of services, others specialise in particular areas.

The free publication *Finding an Agency* is a thorough guide to choosing an agency and it can be found on the IPA website (*www.ipa.co.uk/content/best-practice-guides*). It was created by the five key trade and consultative bodies for the advertising, marketing and public relations industries:

- DMA – Direct Mail Association (*www.dma.org.uk*)
- IPA – Institute of Practitioners In Advertising (*www.ipa.co.uk*)
- ISBA – Incorporated Society of British Advertisers (*www.isba.org.uk*)
- MCCA – Marketing Communication Consultants Organisation (*www.mcca.org.uk*)
- PRCA – Public Relation Consultants Association (*www.prca.org.uk*)

It is a comprehensive 100-page document that sets out the key components of best practice and includes guidelines on the process of searching for and selecting agencies and managing client-agency relationships.

TOP FIVE TIPS FOR CHOOSING AN AGENCY

1 – Decide What Type of Agency You Want

Do you want help with direct mail, your website, your PR? Or are you looking for a combination of skills? Being clear about the type of help you want will help you to focus on companies that specialise in your area(s) of need.

A freelancer who has specialist skills such as graphic design could be more cost-effective than an agency. Freelancers are a viable option and can be good if you are working to a budget. However, if you have a particularly large project, consider their resources and ask yourself whether one person has the capacity to deliver your requirements and if they have all the skills required.

2 – Do Your Research

Once you have established the type of help you need, do some research: talk to colleagues in the industry, find out who they would recommend; visit professional association websites and look up their members; try your local Chamber of Commerce; do a web search for agencies or freelancers in your area.

List the agencies that interest you and look up their websites to find out about their portfolio of clients. Ask yourself if their work reflects the type of approach you are looking for. Call and ask them to send you information about what they do; talk to them about the kind of clients they work with.

With all this information to hand, narrow your list down to two or three who you would like to see to find out more. When you call to arrange a meeting, let them know you will send them a copy of the brief in advance. Explain that this isn't a pitch - you just want to explain your requirements so that you can have a more meaningful discussion about your project at the meeting.

3 – Write A Brief

Before you meet each of the agencies or freelancers, write a brief for your project and send it to them in advance. Remember, you are not asking them to pitch; you are just being clear from the outset about what you want to achieve. This ensures time is not wasted on either side.

4 – Evaluate The Agency

During the meeting to discuss the brief, consider using the following questions to understand more about how the agency or freelancer works. It is important to find out everything you want to know at this meeting, so if they have a PowerPoint presentation, ask them to present it at the end.

Approach & Design Process
- How do they approach creativity, from initial brief to presentation to the client?
- What are the internal design processes that ensure the client gets the best possible design solution?
- Do they have any specific methodologies for the creative process?
- How would they approach the brief you have provided?

Project/Account Management
- Who will be the key point of contact for your company - the person working on the designs or an account manager?
- How do they manage client deadlines?

Costs
- Are the amounts quoted in the proposal full and final?
- Are amendments included in their costs? If so, how many and what type?
- What other costs could be included – eg stock images, photography?
- How would they notify you if there were extra charges?

Existing Clients
- Ask for the names of two or three existing clients you could talk to about their approach and how they work?

Why Would They Like To Work With You?
- Ask why they would like to work with your company and what interests them about the project. This is a great question: their answer will reveal what they know about your company and whether they have taken time to research you and what you do.

Questions

Give them an opportunity to ask questions about the project – it should be a two-way process.

Team Thoughts

During the meeting, get your team to make general notes on their approach, and whether you think you could work with them. Do you like them? Can you see a long-term relationship developing? Are they friendly and approachable? Will they hit deadlines? Could they be the partner you are looking for?

5 – Make Your Selection

You have seen two or three agencies, discussed the brief and found out their inside leg measurement. Now you need to decide which one you want to work with. You may have already discounted two of them, so the choice is easy. However, if you still can't make a decision, remember that you are looking for a partner to work with, so things like the knowledge of the person working on your account or the approach they take to working with clients will be important. Visualise working with them; ask yourself: "How would it feel?"

You want the agency or freelancer to help your business grow and develop, so take the time to find the right partner. You want someone who is able to understand your products and what you are really selling and be able to communicate your messages effectively to your target audience.

13. Don't Forget Sales

"The fact is, everyone is in sales, whatever area you work in, you have clients and you need to sell stuff to them."
JAY ABRAHAM

Although this book covers B2B marketing techniques, we are well aware that marketing doesn't happen in isolation and that to make money you need to make sales. We use this shop analogy to describe how we believe marketing works.

Your marketing activities will get individuals to come through the door of your shop. However, once they are in there, you must have an effective sales process to convert this interest into a sale. As mentioned in previous chapters, getting people to respond to your direct mail and visit your website is great, but you must make the effort to follow up each and every lead into your company, otherwise your marketing efforts will have been wasted.

If sales appointments are to be generated through marketing, a focused approach to sales will be necessary. To maximise these opportunities, time should be set aside for business development and you should develop a sales process that doesn't allow any leads to fall though the cracks.

Whether you have a large sales team or just one person, you need to know what is happening to every lead generated through your marketing campaigns. We have devised a simple sales process that defines when to input information into the database and suggests marketing material to use at each stage.

Of course, your sales process may be very different, but this will give you an idea of the flow of a lead through to a closed sale. Even if you already have a dedicated sales team, take time to make sure the transition between marketing and sales is as smooth as possible and that every marketing lead is followed up. If you don't have a dedicated salesperson or team, consider how you will follow up leads. Whether you do it yourself or use an external agency, make sure it gets done. It would be a shame, after all the effort you have put into bringing leads to your door, for the prospect to find no one in the shop to help them.

SIMPLE SALES PROCESS

Here is a sample sales process that you can use as a basis for yours. You might need more steps or fewer - just be sure to consider what is required at each stage.

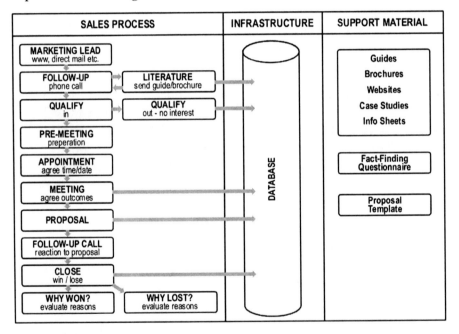

If you have little or no experience of sales and want to read more, these books are simple and informative, easy to read and full of tips on how to sell successfully.

- *Advanced Selling Strategies* – Brian Tracy
- *25 Sales Mistakes and How to Avoid Them* – Stephen Schiffman
- *Successful Selling in a Week* – Christine Harvey
- *Telephone Skills Pocket Book* – Mary Richards
- *Telesales Pocket Book* – Peter Wyllie

14. What To Measure?

*"Measure what is measurable, and
make measurable what is not so."*
GALILEO

You can and should measure the effectiveness of your marketing campaigns. If you want solid facts and figures, these return on investment (ROI) calculations can be used for exhibitions, seminars direct mail and email.

Response Rate

$$\frac{\text{NUMBER OF RESPONSES}}{\text{NUMBER OF DIRECT MAILS}} \quad = \quad \text{RESPONSE RATE}$$

$$\frac{200}{5,000} \quad = \quad 0.04 \ (4\%)$$

Cost Per Lead

$$\frac{\text{COST OF DIRECT MAIL}}{\text{NUMBER OF RESPONSES}} \quad = \quad \text{COST PER LEAD}$$

$$\frac{£3,000}{200} \quad = \quad £15$$

But what do these figures really tell you? You had a good response rate and it cost £15 per lead. Take it a step further and work out the conversion rate from the number of leads into sales.

Conversion Rate

$$\frac{\text{NUMBER OF SALES}}{\text{NUMBER OF LEADS}} = \text{CONVERSION RATE}$$

$$\frac{20}{200} = 0.10\ (10\%)$$

If you know what your average order value is, you can begin to work out what the likely ROI is on any campaign for a particular product as follows.

Complete ROI

DIRECT MAILS SENT OUT	=	5,000
COST OF DIRECT MAIL	=	£3,000
RESPONSE RATE OF 4%	=	200 LEADS
COST PER LEAD	=	£15
CONVERSION RATE OF 10%	=	20 SALES
AVERAGE ORDER VALUE	=	£1,500
TOTAL OF SALES	=	£30,000
ROI	=	900%

As you can see, this would have been a great marketing investment. The initial £3,000 resulted in £30,000 worth of sales and it confirms the direct mail or email campaign was a success.

OTHER MEASUREMENTS

Measuring other marketing activities can be a little more difficult, but we have provided some ways for you to understand how effective other marketing activities might be.

Advertising

Calculating the ROI on advertising using the methods outlined on the previous page can give pretty dismal results - the cost per lead is usually high and the ROI can appear quite low. Remember, in the B2B world, advertising isn't a big lead generation tool; B2B marketing is more about raising awareness and creating a profile for your products, services and brand. You could use this method to find out how many clients your advertising would need to attract for you to break-even:

| TOTAL COST OF ADVERTISING PER YEAR | = | £25,000 |
| AVERAGE SALE OR REVENUE PER CLIENT PER YEAR | = | £1,500 |

Therefore...

| NUMBER OF CLIENTS NEEDED TO BREAK EVEN | = | 16.6 |

PR

It can be very difficult to measure the efficacy of PR. Some companies measure column inches, others what the equivalent space in advertising would have cost them. It is difficult to get a solid ROI on PR. However, what you can do is try to get consistent coverage month on month and use a simple system to measure this. One method we have used is a points system: simply assess your press cuttings and internet news on a monthly basis and allocate points based on the content:

- 1 point: Headline with your company name in it
- 1 point: Image related to your company, person or product
- 1 point: Key message communicated
- 1 point: Quote included
- 1 point: Contact details or website address included
- 1 point: Whole article about your company

By using this system, you will see patterns begin to emerge. You might have a consistent score of around 20 points per month. If this figures starts to fall, you need to find out why and work out where you need to make improvements.

And Finally...

*"Our success has been built on partnerships
from the very beginning."*
BILL GATES

This book gives you all the tools, ideas and skills you need to be an effective B2B marketer, but don't feel you have to do it all on your own. There are a range of agencies that specialise in direct mail, advertising, SEO, etc, that can help you achieve your marketing objectives and give you even more detailed specialist knowledge than we could cover in this book.

Don't be afraid to ask for help. As marketing managers, we worked with a range of agencies to ensure we delivered highly effective marketing campaigns. We worked with them to help us achieve our marketing objectives and in many cases found a partner and ally we could depend on to deliver highly effective marketing activities for us.

You can always contact us for further help and advice and to benefit from our one-to-one marketing coaching programmes - just log on to *www.brightermarketing.com* to find out more.

Further Reading

22 Immutable Laws of Branding – Al and Laura Ries - 978-0006531296

25 Sales Mistakes and How to Avoid Them – Stephen Schiffman - 978-1593160845

Advanced Selling Strategies – Brian Tracy – 978-0684824741

Focus, The Power of Targeted Thinking – Jurgen Wolff – 978-0273715443

Guerrilla Marketing – Jay Conrad Levinson – 978-0749928117

Jelly Effect, How to Make Your Communications Stick – Andy Bounds – 978-1841127606

Love is the Killer App: How to Win Business and Influence Friends Tim Sanders – 978-1400046836

More Words that Sell – Richard Bayan – 978-0071418539

Phrases That Sell: The Ultimate Phrase Finder to Help You Promote Your Products, Services & Ideas – Edward W. Werz and Sally Germain – 978-0809229772

Positioning: The Battle for you Mind – Al Ries and Jack Trout – 978-0071373586

Successful Selling in a Week – Christine Harvey – 978-0340705384

Telephone Skills Pocket Book – Mary Richards – 978-1903776841

Telesales Pocket Book – Peter Wyllie – 978-1870471398

Thinker Toys – Michael Michalko – 978-1580087735

Words that Sell: More Than 6,000 Entries to Help You Promote Your Products, Services, and Ideas – Richard Bayan – 978-0071467858

YES! 50 Secrets from the Science of Persuasion – Robert B. Cialdini, Noah J. Goldstein and Steve J. Martin – 978-1846680168

The Gorillas Want Bananas: The Lean Marketing Bible for Small Expert Businesses – D. Jenkins and J. Gregory – 978-0954568108

Bare Knuckle Selling – S. Hazeldine – 978-1905430055

Bare Knuckle Customer Service – S. Hazeldine, C. Norton – 978-1905430352

Web Links & Resources

DATABASE LISTS

www.marketingfile.com - Marketing File

www.electricmarketing.co.uk - Electric Marketing

www.laingbuisson.co.uk - Laing and Buisson

www.binleys.com - Binleys

www.themanufacturer.com/database - The Manufacturing Database

www.vnuone-to-one.co.uk - VNU One-to-One

www.mardev.com - Mardev

EMAIL CAMPAIGN SOFTWARE

www.livewirecampaign.com

www.dotmailer.co.uk

www.newzapp.co.uk

www.aweber.com

www.icontact.com

www.infusionsoft.com

www.constantcontact.com

PR & PRESS RELEASES

www.prwebdirect.com/pressreleasetips.php

MAGAZINE AND NEWSPAPER CIRCULATION FIGURES

www.abc.org.uk – Audit Bureau of Circulation, UK

www.accessabc.com – Audit Bureau, US

FREELANCE DIRECTORY

www.elance.com – Freelancers in a range of disciplines

SUBMITTING ARTICLES

www.ezinearticles.com

www.submityourarticle.com

POWERPOINT PRESENTATIONS

www.m62.net – Tips on PowerPoint presentations

GOOGLE ALGORITHM

www.uspto.gov – Patents website

www.seomoz.org/article/google-historical-data-patent - Interpretation of the algorithm.

SEARCH ENGINE OPTIMISATION RESOURCES

www.searchengineguide.com – Information and tips for beginners, especially around keywords.

www.searchengineworkshops.com/seo-tip-of-the-day.html – Sign up to receive an SEO tip every day.

www.seobook.com – Lots of free SEO resources as well as PPC information. SEO tools that enable you to check how your website is ranked, etc, can be found at *http://tools.seobook.com*.

www.wordtracker.com – To help you understand how many people are searching for a particular search term and how effective it would be. This is the paid-for version and has much more functionality than the free one which can be found at *http://freekeywords.wordtracker.com*.

www.futurenowinc.com/wewe.htm - Checks your website for customer-focused copy.

www.iwebtool.com/spider_view – Search engine spider simulator.

www.webconfs.com/keyword-density-checker.php – Keyword density checker.

http://toolbar.google.com – Google toolbar which includes extra information such as a website's page rank.

www.webferret.com – Use this to find all the sites linked to a particular site.

www.webconfs.com/reciprocal-link-checker.php – Checks your website's links are working.

www.marketleap.com/publinkpop – Reviews the popularity of your links compared to other sites.

www.google.com/webmaster/tools - Suite of tools from Google to help you build search engine-friendly websites.

www.w3.org – International consortium that sets web standards and guidelines.

BLOGGING SITES

www.typepad.com – business-focused

www.wordpress.com – business-focused

www.blogger.com – free and more for personal use, but can work for a business.

BLOGGING CONSULTANTS – WILL SET BLOGS UP FOR YOU

www.businessblogangel.com – UK-based

www.stevewatsononline.com – UK-based

http://michaelmartine.com/blog-consulting - US-based, includes free e-book that has a 12-step process for starting a business blog.

GOOGLE PAY-PER-CLICK

www.perrymarshall.com – Definitive guide to Google PPC.

https://adwords.google.com - Tutorials information to help you set up your Adword campaign.

www.seobook.com/overture-adwords.pdf - Overview of PPC.

www.spyfu.com – Find out what keywords and phrases your competitors are bidding for.

Adword Accelerator *www.adwordaccelerator.com* and

Adword Analayzer *www.adwordanalyzer.com* – Provide extra information for Google Ad campaigns.

https://adwords.google.com/select/KeywordToolExternal – The free Google Adword analyser tool.

https://adwords.google.co.uk/select/TrafficEstimatorSandbox – estimate the price required to rank number one on Adwords for 85% of the time.

www.google.com/websiteoptimizer - Tells you which of your landing pages is likely to work better and tests them in real time.

www.writeppcads.com – How to write successful Google adverts.

www.google.com/analytics – Gives statistics on your campaigns, helps you write better ads, strengthen your marketing.

SEO AND PPC COMPANIES

www.simplifyinternetmarketing.co.uk – UK-based

www.simplifytheinternet.com – UK-based

www.bruceclay.com or *www.bruceclay.co.uk* – UK and US-based

FINDING AN AGENCY

www.ipa.co.uk/content/best-practice-guides - created by the five key trade and consultative bodies for the advertising, marketing and public relations industries:

- DMA – Direct Mail Association – *www.dma.org.uk*
- IPA – Institute of Practitioners In Advertising – *www.ipa.co.uk*
- ISBA – Incorporated Society of British Advertisers – *www.isba.org.uk*
- MCCA – Marketing Communication Consultants Organisation – *www.mcca.org.uk*
- PRCA – Public Relation Consultants Association – *www.prca.org.uk*

About The Authors

JOANNE MORLEY

Joanne has over 15 years of marketing experience at a range of companies including ICL, Tesco, Allasso, Integralis. Joanne began her professional career in Marketing at ICL, where she developed successful reseller marketing programmes to enable resellers to sell IT products and services across the UK. Joanne still credits her 'first job' as the place where she became interested in, and gleaned her understanding of, marketing strategy, hierarchy and employee motivation.

Throughout the technology boom of the early 90's, Joanne held senior in-house roles for a selection of leading internet security companies, including Integralis and Allasso. Here she implemented successful marketing, and business growth programmes and developed strategies for cross-platform campaigns which led to some of the most successful direct-mail response results in both companies history.

In 1999 Joanne was Head of Marketing for start-up company Allasso, as part of a four-man management team, where she developed a successful marketing strategy which focused on PR as the core tool to gain recognition in the new internet security marketplace. Within two years, her strategies had assisted in helping the company to a £10M+ PA turnover.

After years working in high pressure marketing roles, Joanne felt the need for a change and established Brighter Marketing in 2002 with a business colleague Siobhan Lees to develop a unique coaching based approach to marketing. Working with a range of businesses they have helped transform the marketing approach in SMEs and large organisations in the UK.

Joanne has a single-minded focus, which allows her to dissect and fully understand the strategic implications faced by each of her clients – whatever their field. She likes to do things properly – a trait that leads back to her days as a child working for her parent's guesthouse business. "I would say that I have a passion for making sure things are done right. I like developing creative marketing strategies that meet the needs of our clients' and will solely focus on each project until I know we've got it absolutely right for them and am confident the tactics will deliver the agreed results."

SIOBHAN LEES

Siobhan Lees has over 20 years of marketing and business development experience and has held senior positions at a selection of Europe's leading technology and retail companies, including Marks & Spencer, Cable & Wireless, Energis and Demon Internet.

Siobhan's professional career began at Marks & Spencer as a Management Trainee where she took full advantage of the leading retailer's training scheme, developing an in-depth understanding of the retail industry. In the following eight years Siobhan worked across a variety of departments, including Fashion, Outside Warehousing and Cost-Control.

In 1990 Siobhan was approached by Thorn UK (later Radio Rentals) where she took on the role of District Manager before being promoted to Regional Manager, overseeing the leading the stores 98 outlets in London and the South East of England. During her time here, Siobhan collected numerous awards for her strategic direction in the areas of sales, performance, people development and standards.

After meeting Joanne through business, Siobhan realised that they both had a passion for marketing and business development, but weren't reaching their potential in the organisations they were working for. So after some brainstorming and a few glasses of wine, Brighter Marketing was born in 2002 with the goal of helping organisations transform the way the marketed their products and services.

Siobhan has always had a passion for developing excitement and, in turn, passion and confidence in her team members. She sees this as one of the key elements in the success of Brighter Marketing: "When we work on any piece of activity, Joanne and I really believe in the people we are working with which and get a buzz out of transferring the practical marketing and business development skills they need to give them the business they want."

◯ brightermarketing

Brighter Marketing is a marketing company focused on business to business marketing solutions that deliver results. We are not just another agency or a design company offering some marketing consultancy. We can offer real life marketing help and advice that will make a massive difference to the results you get from your marketing.

What you don't know could be costing you a fortune in mis-placed adverts, ineffective direct mail or marketing that isn't generating results! So if you have want to make a big difference to the way you market your business, take action NOW.

We can definitely help you unlock your marketing potential, so take the first step to success visit our website *www.brightermarketing.com* and learn how our marketing solutions can give you the business you want. Here are just some of the ways we can help you :

- **One-to-one marketing coaching** – we transfer the skills you need to make your marketing a success
- **Strategic marketing advice** – we work with you to develop realistic plans that will help you to grow your business
- **Marketing Creativity** – if you need to inject some creativity into your marketing then we can help you unlock your marketing potential with creative workshops
- **Articles and help** – visit our website and get access to marketing articles or subscribe to our marketing tips.

www.brightermarketing.com

THE GORILLAS WANT BANANAS

The Lean Marketing™ Handbook for Small Expert Businesses

DOING BUSINESS

WINNING BUSINESS

GETTING PAID

DEBBIE JENKINS & JOE GREGORY

www.gorillaswantbananas.com

BARE KNUCKLE
SELLING

KNOCKOUT SALES TACTICS THEY WON'T TEACH YOU AT BUSINESS SCHOOL

SIMON HAZELDINE
FOREWORD BY DR. JOE VITALE

www.bookshaker.com

Lightning Source UK Ltd.
Milton Keynes UK
06 September 2009
143368UK00002B/43/P